Trübner's Oriental Series

THE CLASSICAL POETRY OF THE JAPANESE

Trübner's Oriental Series

JAPAN
In 3 Volumes

I	The Classical Poetry of the Japanese *Basil Hall Chamberlain*
II	Discovery of Japanese Idealism *Kishio Satomi*
III	Japanese Civilization *Kishio Satomi*

THE CLASSICAL POETRY OF THE JAPANESE

BASIL HALL CHAMBERLAIN

Routledge
Taylor & Francis Group
LONDON AND NEW YORK

First published in 1880 by
Trübner & Co Ltd

Reprinted in 2000, 2002 by
Routledge
2 Park Square, Milton Park, Abingdon, Oxon, OX14 4RN

Simultaneously published in the USA and Canada by Routledge

711 Third Avenue, New York, NY 10017

Transferred to Digital Printing 2007

Routledge is an imprint of the Taylor & Francis Group

First issued in paperback 2013

British Library Cataloguing in Publication Data
A CIP catalogue record for this book
is available from the British Library

The Classical Poetry of the Japanese

ISBN 978-0-415-24532-6 (hbk)
ISBN 978-0-415-86584-5 (pbk)

THE CLASSICAL POETRY

OF

THE JAPANESE.

BY

BASIL HALL CHAMBERLAIN,

AUTHOR OF

"*YEIGO HEÑKAKU ICHIRAÑ.*"

LONDON:

TRÜBNER & CO., LUDGATE HILL.

1880.

PREFACE.

In bringing before the public a subject which, if remote, has at least the merit of novelty, it is the translator's pleasant duty to acknowledge the assistance which has done much to smooth for him the difficulties of an almost untrodden path. From European sources, indeed, little or no help has been derived. But to a native man of letters, Suzuki Tsunemasa, thanks are due for continued aid and counsel during the preparation of the present versions, while the necessary preliminary studies would never have been successfully carried through but for the kind encouragement of the aged poetess Tachibana-no-Toseko. Writing at a distance from England, and unable personally to supervise the correction of the proofs, the translator must beg the indulgence of Orientalists if any errors should have crept into the spelling of Japanese words. A few of the "Short Odes" and three or four of the longer pieces have already appeared in the pages either of the "Cornhill Magazine" or of the "Transactions of the Asiatic Society of Japan," and to the President and Council of this Society and to the Editor of that Magazine thanks are due for permission to republish. The chief native works that have been consulted are :—

Hiyaku-Niñ Itsu-Shiu Hito-Yo Gatari ("Nightly Conversations on the Hundred Odes by a Hundred Poets"), by Wozaki Motoyoshi.

Ise Mono-Gatari Ko-I ("The Old Signification of the Talc of Ise"), by Kamo-no-Mabuchi.

Kagura Iri-Aya ("The Damask of the Sacred Songs Penetrated"), by Tachibana-no-Moribe.

Kita Riu Yeukiyoku Boñ ("Book of Lyric Dramas According to the Kita Style").

Kokiñ Wa-Ka Shifu Uchi-Giki ("Memoranda Concerning the Collection of Japanese Odes Ancient and Modern"), by Kamo-no-Mabuchi.

Kozhiki Deñ ("Traditional Commentary on the Records of Antiquity"), by Motowori Norinaga.

Kuwañze Riu Yeukiyoku Boñ ("Book of Lyric Dramas According to the Kuwañze Style").

Kuwañzhi Kau ("Considerations on the Pillow-Words"), by Kamo-no-Mabuchi.

Mañyefu Kau ("Considerations on the Myriad Leaves"), by Kamo-no-Mabuchi.

Mañyefu Kau Betsuki ("Addenda to the Considerations on the Myriad Leaves"), by Kamo-no-Mabuchi.

Mañyefu Shifu-Ho Seu ("Gleanings from the Myriad Leaves,—a Commentary"), by Kitamura Kigiñ.

Mañyefushifu Riyakuge ("Abbreviated Commentary on the Collection of a Myriad Leaves"), by Tachibana-no Chikage.

Miyako Meishiyo Dzuwe ("Illustrations of the Sights of the Capital"), by Magakizhima Akisato.

Mo-Shio Gusa ("Seaweed"), by Souseki.

Nihoñ Shiyoki ("Notices of Japan"), by Prince Toneri.

Nou Kiyau-Geñ ("Comic Interludes of the Lyric Dramas"), M.S.

Setsutsu Meishiyo Dzuwe ("Illustrations of the Sights of Setsutsu"), by Magakizhima Akisato.

Shimotsuke Koku-Shi ("Archives of the Province of Shimotsuke"), by Kahano Morihiro.

Shiñ-Señ Sei-Shi Roku ("Newly Selected Index of Family Names"), by Prince Mata.

Utahi Sakushiya Nou Butai Tou Kaki-Tsuke ("Memoranda Concerning Dramatic Authors, the Lyric Stage, &c."), by the Heads of the Nou Families, M.S.

Wa-Miyau Ruwi-Zhiu Seu ("Japanese Words Collected in Categories with Commentary"), by Minamoto-no Shitagafu.

Yamato Meishiyo Dzuwe ("Illustrations of the Sights of Yamato"), by Hairañ.

Yamato Mono-Gatari Seu ("Commentary on the Tales of Japan"), by Kitamura Kigiñ.

Yeukiyoku Shifu-Yefu Seu ("Gleanings from the Lyric Dramas,—a Commentary"), by Zhiñkou.

IMPERIAL NAVAL COLLEGE, YEDO,
September 1880.

CONTENTS.

ELEGIES.

MISCELLANEOUS POEMS.

SHORT STANZAS.

SELECTIONS.

APPENDICES.

THE CLASSICAL POETRY

OF

THE JAPANESE.

INTRODUCTION.

I.

THE current impression that the Japanese are a nation of imitators is in the main correct. As they copy us to-day, so did they copy the Chinese and Coreans a millennium and a half ago. Religion, philosophy, laws, administration, written characters, all arts but the very simplest, all science, or at least what then went by that name,—everything was imported from the neighbouring continent; so much so, that of all that we are accustomed to term "Old Japan" scarce one trait in a hundred is really and properly Japanese. Not only are their silk and lacquer not theirs by right of invention, nor their painting (albeit so often praised by European critics for its originality), nor their porcelain, nor their music, but even the larger part of their language consists of mispronounced Chinese; and from the Chinese they have drawn new names for already existing places, and new titles for their ancient gods. That their literature should be, for the most part, fashioned on the Chinese model and express Chinese ideas is, therefore, but what was *à priori* to be expected. What was not to be looked for, was, that one whole branch of that literature should, weathering the storm that shook its infancy, have preserved down to our own times the unaltered form and the almost unaltered substance of the earliest manifestation of Japanese thought. This one original product of the Japanese mind is the native poetry.

So remarkable a fact should, of itself, suffice to gain for the poetry of this people the first place in the attention of those who make Japan and Japanese the special object of their investigations. It should even attract the passing notice of the more general reader, who, in the present day, has to peruse quite a library of books treating of Japan,—and this, altogether apart from any intrinsic merit which that poetry may or may not possess. Hitherto, like the rest of the literature of the far East, it has been more often judged than studied. The following pages are an attempt to make the study more general, by placing it within the reach of those who, while sharing in the interest for Japan now universally felt, are yet not prepared to face the difficulties which must ever continue to hedge in the Oriental originals.

In order to appreciate the assertion made as to the peculiar and non-Chinese character of the *form* of Japanese poetry,—in other words, of its prosody,—it is, of course, necessary to possess some knowledge of the distinguishing features of Chinese versification, a subject which it does not fall within the scope of this work, as a popular one, to treat in any detail. Suffice it to say that, as in French verse, so in Chinese, rhyme is considered essential, but that the syllables of which each line is composed, instead of being, as in French, merely counted, must follow each other according to rule in various tones, just as the cadence of an English verse is determined not merely by the rhyme, and by the enumeration of the syllables composing each line, but also by the relative position of the accented syllables and those on which no stress is laid. The third chief characteristic of Chinese versification is what has been termed "parallelism," that is, the exact correspondence between every word in two successive lines or clauses, noun for noun, verb for verb, particle for particle, thus—

> *We-would-keep the-Spring, but-the-Spring*
> *will-not stay: the-Spring goeth, and-men*
> *are-forlorn and-lonely.*
> *We-would-avert the-Wind, but-the-Wind*
> *will-not be-at-peace: the-Wind riseth,*
> *and-the-blossoms are-stricken and-desolated.**

Owing to the unrivalled conciseness of the Chinese literary style, all the words bracketed together in the above, form but one character, that is, one syllable, and the correspondence is, therefore, as exact in sound as it is in sense.

The structure of a great portion of Hebrew poetry rests on a somewhat looser kind of parallelism. Take, for instance, Psalm cxiv.—

* Verses by Peh Kü-Yih, a famous poet of the T'ang dynasty, who died A.D. 846.

When Israel came out of Egypt: and the house of Jacob from among the strange people,
Judah was his sanctuary: and Israel his dominion.
The sea saw that and fled: Jordan was driven back.
The mountains skipped like rams: and the little hills like young sheep.
&c. &c.

Of all such complications Japanese prosody knows nothing. It regards neither rhyme, tone, accent, quantity, nor alliteration, nor does its rather frequent parallelism follow any regular method. Its only essential rule is that every poem must consist of alternate lines of five and seven syllables, with, generally, an extra line of seven syllables to mark the close. It is, indeed, prosody reduced to its simplest expression.* Yet so little artifice is needed to raise

* Here is an example. It is the original of the elegy on p. 71, beginning "Alas! poor mortal maid"—

5. *Utsusemishi*
7. *Kami ni taheneba,*
5. *Hanare-wite,*
7. *Asa nageku kimi;*
5. *Sakari-wite,*
7. *Waga kofuru kimi*
5. *Tama naraba,*
7. *Te ni maki-mochite;*
5. *Kinu naraba,*
7. *Nugu toki mo naku,*
5. *Waga kohimu*
7. *Kimi zo kizo no yo*
7. *Ime ni miyetsuru.*

The fondness of the Japanese for brevity has led them to write an immense amount of poetry in a very short stanza of thirty-one syllables, thus—

5. *Momiji-ba wo*
7. *Kaze ni makasete*
5. *Miru yori mo,*
7. *Hakanaki mono ha*
7. *Inochi nari keri.*

Some European writers have falsely supposed that the flights of the Japanese Muse were always bound down within these lilliputian limits. For a translation of the above stanza see p. 129 (No. 38).

prose to verse in this most musical of tongues, that such a primitive metre still satisfies the native ear to-day in every street-ballad, as it already did in the seventh century at the Mikado's court; and no serious attempt has ever been made to alter it in the slightest degree, even during the period of the greatest intellectual ascendancy of China.

Though not essential, there are, however, some usual additions to the means at the Japanese versifier's command. They are three in number, and altogether original, viz., what are styled "Pillow-words," "Prefaces," and "Pivots."

The "Pillow-words" are meaningless expressions which are prefixed to other words merely for the sake of euphony. Almost every word of note has some "Pillow-word" on which it may, so to speak, rest its head; and dictionaries of them are often resorted to by the unready Japanese versifier, just as rhyming dictionaries come to the aid of the poetasters of modern Europe.

A "Preface" is but a "Pillow-word" on a more extensive scale, consisting, as it does, of a whole sentence prefixed to a poem, not on account of any connection with the sense of what follows, but merely as an introduction pleasing to the ear. This ornament is chiefly confined to the very early poetry, whereas the "Pillow-words" have flourished equally in every age.

The "Pivot" is a more complicated device, and one which, in any European language, would be not only insupportable, but impossible, resting, as it does, on a most peculiar kind of *jeu de mots*. A word having two significations serves as a species of hinge on which two doors turn, so that while the first part of the poetical phrase has no logical end, the latter part has no logical beginning. They run into each other, and the sentence could not possibly be construed. To the English reader such a punning invention will doubtless seem the height of misapplied ingenuity, calculated to reduce poetry to the level of the acrostic and the *bouts rimés.* But, as a matter of fact, the impression produced by these linked verses is delightful in the extreme, passing, as they do, before the reader, like a series of dissolving views, vague, graceful, and suggestive. The Japanese, too, have their acrostics, and also their common puns, with the same stigma of vulgarity as is attached by ourselves to such lower sallies of wit; but the line between them and the poetical artifice just described, though difficult to define, is very sharply drawn. It rests, probably, chiefly on the fact that newness is an essential constituent of the ludicrous sensation excited by the *jeu de mots* properly so called, which newness forms no part of the "Pivot," it being, as a rule, in all poems the same half-dozen words that serve as the points of transition from clause to clause. This ornament especially characterises the old poetical dramas, and renders them a peculiarly arduous study to such as do not thoroughly appreciate its nature.*

So much for the independent character of the *form* of Japanese poetry. To prove conclusively that its

* Those who may feel curious for more details on the subject of Japanese prosody should consult Aston's "Grammar of the Japanese Written Language." For a special essay on the "Pillow-words," &c., the present writer may be allowed to refer to a paper printed in the fifth volume of the "Transactions of the Asiatic Society of Japan."

substance is equally autochthonous would be a harder task, though few, probably, of those competent to form an opinion on the point would deny that such is the case. Three facts may, however, be signalised as tending to show that such likenesses as do exist,—for instance, the absence of impersonation, and the very secondary place taken by the religious element,—should be attributed rather to a fundamental resemblance between the Chinése and the Altaic minds than to any direct influence of the former upon the latter.

In the first place, it seems scarcely doubtful that the earliest Japanese poetical compositions that have come down to us date from an age preceding the introduction of the art of writing, or at least its general diffusion, and when, consequently, the study of Chinese literary models was, if not impossible, unlikely in the extreme.* Moreover, the earliest general teachers of Chinese learning were the Buddhist missionaries, who, we may presume, esteemed true doctrine much more highly than they did *belles lettres*, while the stray merchants, adventurers, and outlaws who preceded them, are still less likely to have thought of meddling with, or to have been able to inspire, the songs of either court or people. Yet in all essential respects the earliest poems resemble those produced by the bards of succeeding ages, when Chinese influence undoubtedly deeply swayed the national mind. Were this fact altogether indisputable, no further argument

* Tradition places the arrival in Japan of the first Corean teacher in A.D. 284; but there is no reliable evidence to show that the Japanese studied with any profit till the time of the preaching of Buddhism in the sixth century.

would be required. But absolute proof of any assertion regarding so dim a past as that in which began the intercourse between China and Japan being unobtainable, no element of the discussion should be omitted.

Secondly, therefore, it may be stated that such differences of style and spirit as can be traced, clearly show us the more ancient poems as being also the simpler, the more natural, and intrinsically the better, which could scarcely have been the case had their inspiration been derived from abroad; for every copy is a parody, and the most salient peculiarities of the Chinese style would have been the first to be seized on. Then, little by little, the national mind would have shaken itself free from the foreign leading-strings which had guided its first faint efforts, as did, in fact, partially occur in the case of history, philosophy, and essay-writing; and the tenth, eleventh, twelfth, and thirteenth centuries would have been the zenith of Japanese poetry, as they were of Japanese literature in all its other branches. As a matter of fact, however, the sources of true lyric poetry suddenly dried up at the commencement of that epoch. Thenceforward, instead of the heart-outpourings of the older poets, we find nothing but empty prettinesses and conceits, confined within the narrowest limits. The lyric drama, it is true, arose and flourished during the Middle Ages; but, though deeply tinged with Buddhist ideas, and though frequently quoting the Chinese poets, it is still, both in form, treatment, and choice of subjects, distinctly national and indigenous.

Lastly, the originality of the Japanese system of versification, which has been independently established, is in itself a weighty argument in favour of the equal originality of the thoughts which that versification is the means of expressing. In all the instances known to us of a people borrowing its inspiration from abroad, the foreign poetical form has been the first thing to be adopted. The Latins submitted without a groan to the heavy yoke of Greek prosody; the semi-barbarians of Northern Europe adopted the rhymes, as they did the religion, of their Southern neighbours; while in our own days, in like manner, English stanzaic arrangement and English prosodial conventions are following the missionaries into the homes of the numerous uncultured tribes to whom they bring an extraneous civilisation. To this rule Japan shows us a complete contrast, by far the simplest explanation of which is, that her poetry is, in every respect, a plant of native growth. That its substance is very peculiar is by no means what is meant to be asserted. On the contrary, the reader can hardly fail to be struck with its generality and want of local colouring. When, therefore, originality is claimed for this product of Japanese thought, it is merely originality in the sense of spontaneous invention, not originality in the sense of uniqueness.

II.

The classical poetry of the Japanese is contained in the "*Mañyefushifu*," or "Collection of a Myriad Leaves," and in a large number of collections made by imperial order during the tenth, eleventh, twelfth, thirteenth, fourteenth, and fifteenth centuries, and commonly known as the "Collections of the One-and-Twenty Reigns." To these may be added, as quasi-classical, the lyric dramas known by the name of "*Utahi.*"

The "Myriad Leaves," a selection from which forms the chief portion of the following work, are not, indeed, the very oldest lyric compositions of the Japanese; or, to speak more correctly, they were not brought together at quite so early a period as that belonging to the historical books called "*Kozhiki,*" or "Notices of Antiquity," dating from the year 712 of our era, and "*Nihoñgi,*" or "Records of Japan," dating from 720, both containing a considerable number of poems attributed to divine and other legendary personages. These are not, however, commonly included by the Japanese themselves in the cycle of their classical poetry; and, moreover, a complete and literal version of the books in question is so earnestly to be looked for in the interests of Japanese archæology, that it has been thought best not here to trench on ground which would have to be gone over again in a more critical spirit.

The exact date of the bringing together in the twenty volumes * of the "Myriad Leaves" of the productions of the most esteemed poets that had appeared up to that time, though not known with certainty, is referred by the best native critics to the reign of the Mikado Shiyaumu (died A.D. 756). The compiler was a favourite of that monarch, Prince

* Originally twenty small scrolls of a size convenient for rolling and unrolling. As now published, however, with superincumbent masses of commentary, the volumes are tomes indeed.

Moroye (died A.D. 757), to whom some would add as coadjutor the court noble Yakamochi (died A.D. 785), a number of whose poems are contained in the latter volumes of the collection. It has, however, been suggested that only the volumes now bearing the numbers I., II., XI., XII., XIII., and XIV. should be regarded as forming the original compilation, the remaining fourteen having been added a few years later from various private sources. Those to whom Japanese is familiar, will find the whole matter treated *in extenso*, in Mabuchi's edition of the "Myriad Leaves;" but to the general reader, and, indeed, to the main question of authenticity and antiquity, it matters little what decision be arrived at on this and other minor points. There are no grounds for placing the *composition* of any of the poems later than A.D. 760, while from the beginning of the tenth century onwards, that is, from less than a hundred and fifty years after that date, we have constant and unimpeachable reference to the collection as a body, and to its appearance during the period when Nara was the capital of the country, viz. (including temporary migrations of the court to other towns in the neighbourhood), from A.D. 710 to 784. Knowing, moreover, as we do, the language of the tenth century, the linguistic test alone would suffice to throw back a century or two the composition of the most modern of the "*Mañyefushifu*" odes, while for by far the greater number a much higher antiquity may, on the same grounds, be claimed.

The "*Kokiñshifu*," or "Collection of Odes Ancient and Modern," the first of the "Collections of the One-and-Twenty Reigns," was compiled in the year 905 by the high-born poet Tsurayuki and three coadjutors. It consists almost entirely of the short thirty-one-syllable stanzas, of which a specimen was given in the footnote to page 4. This stanza, after having, during the ages that witnessed the production of the poems contained in the old histories and in the "Myriad Leaves," struggled against the longer form which was then also in common use, drove the latter out of the field, and has ever since remained the favourite metre of a people, who, in every species of composition, consider brevity to be the soul of wit. The many thousands of stanzas forming this collection, are arranged, according to their subjects, under the headings of Spring, Summer, Autumn, Winter, Congratulations, Parting, Travelling, Acrostics, Love, Elegies, Various, Conceits, and one or two minor ones, several of these headings being themselves subdivided for the sake of convenience of reference. Thus, Love is broken up into five parts, commencing with Love Unconfessed, and ending with Love Unrequited and Forgotten. Such a conceit is highly characteristic of the downward tendency of the Japanese mind since the simpler and healthier early days, and of the substitution of hair-splitting puerilities for the true spirit of poetry. So far as they go, however, the "Odes Ancient and Modern" are not without manifold charms, and are decidedly superior to the twenty imperial collections that succeeded them, for which reason a small selection of representative short stanzas has been made from them alone.

Though fading, the poetical spirit of the country did not, however, yet wither completely away. Indeed, some may think that, like the forests of the land that gave it birth, it was fairer in its autumn tints than in its summer or in its spring. Towards the end of the fourteenth century, in the hands of the Buddhist priesthood, who during that troublous epoch had become almost the sole repositaries of taste and learning, arose the lyric drama, at first but an adaptation of the old religious dances, the choric songs accompanying which were expanded and improved. The next step was the introduction of individual personages, which led to the adoption of a dramatic unity in the plot, though the supreme importance still assigned to the chorus, left to the performance its mainly lyric character, till, at a somewhat later period, the theatrical tendency became supreme, and the romantic melodrama of the modern Japanese stage was evolved. The last of the four plays translated in this work is a specimen of Japanese classical poetry just before this final step was taken, when the new spirit was already struggling within the old forms. The analogy of the course of development here sketched out with that of the Greek drama is too obvious to need any remark. Great doubt hangs over the precise date and authorship of most of the dramatic pieces, on account of the Japanese custom of attributing to the head of the house of lyric actors at any given time, all the plays brought out under his auspices. But before the end of the sixteenth century their production had ceased, and with them the torch of Japanese inspiration finally became extinct.

Then during the long peace of more than two centuries that preceded the arrival of the American men-of-war in Uraga Bay arose the critical and antiquarian school. Every monastery, every noble's mansion, was ransacked for the written relics that had survived the chances of so many ages of feudal warfare. The pioneers * of this Japanese renaissance inoculated the educated classes with that passion for the literary and religious features of antiquity, which, afterwards extending into the political domain, so greatly contributed to the overthrow of the usurped authority of the Shogunate, and to the re-establishment of the old imperial régime. The ancient language was elucidated, the ancient poets commented on, the ancient style imitated, by men to whom Old Japan was all in all. What might have been the final result had the native mind been left to itself, it is hard to conjecture. Would this small far-Eastern renaissance, after expending its first natural antiquarian energy, have resulted in any new flowering forth of the national genius, or had every possible vein been exhausted, and would the intellect of the country, artificially walled in from the fresh air of the world at large, have revolved for ever in the circle of an arid scholasticism? History, as we know, took an altogether unexpected turn. The sudden influx of Western ideas, checked the natural course of events by introducing a potent novel factor; and the Japanese, at no time given to idealism, have, during the last few years, attached themselves to the pursuit of the advantages of the material side of European civilisation, with an eagerness amounting to disdain for everything poetical, or even literary, in any branch. Some stray volumes of poetry may,

* The names of Mabuchi, Motowori, and others of lesser note, will occur o every student of Japanese literature who is at the same time a lover of purity of style.

indeed, occasionally issue from the press. But they are mostly copies of copies,—imitations either of the mediæval courtly versifiers, who themselves looked to the "Odes Ancient and Modern" for their models, or of the *réchauffé* productions of the last-century revival school. Ancient Japanese verses are now written just as our schoolboys write Latin verses; even the popular songs for the singing and dancing girls being composed in what is, in reality, a dead language mechanically reproduced. Of course this cannot go on for ever. Poetry and *belles lettres* must either perish utterly, or they must adapt themselves to the changed circumstances of the times. But these things are ever harder to alter than are political systems and ways of life, and as yet there is not the slightest indication of what the Japanese poetry of the future will be like; the only thing that may be predicted of it with tolerable certainty is, that its outward form will probably receive less modification than its inward essence.

III.

It is with the past, however, and not with the future, that we are concerned. What were the characteristics, and what is the value of the old standard poetry of Japan?

The answers to these questions may best be found by those who, without any foregone conclusions or special personal interest, will be at the trouble of perusing a sufficient number of representative specimens of the productions of the Japanese Muse. The object here proposed is to render this for the first time possible for English readers, the translations being purposely left to speak, as much as possible, for themselves, unencumbered by any mysterious array of unknown characters, and unaided by any notes but such as are indispensable to full comprehension.* From certain points of view, doubtless, the student who has devoted years of loving toil to the task of saturating himself with the letter and spirit of the originals should be likewise best able to appreciate them. But appreciation and partiality are akin, and all general judgments passed by specialists on the object of their investigations must be open to suspicion. If, therefore, a few such generalities are here made room for, it is not as information that they must be regarded, but simply as suggestions, which it is for the less biassed reader to accept or to disagree with, as his truer judgment may dictate.

It would seem, then, that simplicity, love of precedent, and a certain courtly polish, are the most characteristic features of the poetry of the Japanese, —characteristics which, as the familiar instance of French literature may show us, have a natural affinity for each other, though each one of them may, in the case before us, be easily traced back to its own proper actuating cause.

---

* The only English work on the subject is Mr. Dickins's "*Hyak Niw Is'shiu*," translations of a favourite mediæval collection of thirty-one-syllable stanzas. There is in French a valuable work by the well-known Japanologue, Mons. Léon de Rosny, published under the title of "Anthologie Japonaise," and containing prose versions of a few of the "*Mañye-fushifu*" poems, with critical notes for the benefit of the student of the language.

To take the courtliness first. Its reason lies on the surface. It was in a court that the poetry of Japan sprang up and flourished. Indeed the whole literature may be said to have been written by, and for, a small circle of lords and ladies, princes and princesses, who, when not helping to swell the Mikado's train at Nara, the capital, or at the summer palace of Yoshino, were the bearers of imperial missives to the neighbouring continental monarchs, or the consorts or mothers of viceroys of recently conquered provinces. To this very day a different cast of features distinguishes the high-born Japanese from the common folk, whose "pudding-faces" announce their intellectual inferiority, and who, at that early period, when but little mixture of blood could as yet have taken place, doubtless retained in a still more marked degree the impress of their Aino descent. All talent was, therefore, as naturally aristocratic as was all education,—so much so, that we find in the "*Mañyefushifu*" what reads like a note of surprise at the possibility of poetic genius manifesting itself in any man of plebeian origin.* Thus did it come about that Japanese poetry, though often immoral, was from the very beginning polished and refined. Nowhere do we come across a low word or a vulgar thought. Even the mention of low and vulgar people seems well-nigh prohibited. It is always upward, never downward, that the poet looks, so that if, for instance, a drought is the subject of his verse, he makes lamentation, not for the sufferings of the peasantry, but for the loss to the imperial exchequer!†

* See p. 63. † See p. 111.

Thus, too, we may account for the general avoidance of shocking and over-vivid themes, including the theme of war; for though the Japanese have ever been a military people, and were, indeed, during the earlier classic times, still busily engaged in subduing the remoter portions of their empire, yet murder and bloodshed were not deemed fit subjects to occupy a courtly pen, or to be sung before so refined and sensitive an audience.

It may be, perhaps, in part, to this same aristocratic origin of the poetry, that should be ascribed the love of precedent which distinguishes it. More probably, however, we have here an example of the influence, not of circumstances, but of race. The Japanese lyrists belonged to a court, but that court was an Altaic, a Tartar one. Its members came of a family of nations to whom the spark of genius has been denied, and who must hold fast to the few ideas inherited from their ancestors, if they would not, like the steppes from whence they issued, become altogether barren.

The simplicity which has been noted as the third characteristic (and it is, perhaps, the most marked of the three) is doubtless owing to the same poverty of the intellectual constitution. Acting together with the love of precedent, it confined the vehicle of expression within the limits of one unchanging metre, and it likewise, for nearly a thousand years, forbade all poetical attempts beyond the strictly lyrical domain. Epic, didactic, and satirical poetry are here quite unknown, and the drama was of late growth. Of all such productions as narratives or discussions in a versified form there is likewise no trace, neither do we, as in China, find much taste for poetically cadenced prose. Indeed, the Japanese theory and practice recognise none of those fine distinctions between poetry, and verse, that are often drawn in countries farther to the West. According to their view, all poetry must be in verse, and all verse must be poetical; and their definition of the word "poetical" omits much that is elsewhere considered, not indeed essential, but welcome as an addition. There are no soundings of the depths of the human heart: that would be philosophy, and not poetry; and for philosophy there was no need in the land of the gods, where all men were naturally perfect.* There are no invectives against rulers or aspirations after liberty: † that would be, not poetry, but politics, or rather treason against the heaven-born Mikado, the descendant of the sun. There are, for similar reasons, but few prayers to the upper powers; neither are there, in a country possessing, indeed, a mythology, but no religion properly so called, any yearnings after a possible life beyond the grave. What we find is the expression, in natural language, of the simple feelings common to all mankind,—love, regret, loyalty, attachment to old traditions, and, in the place of religion and of moralising, nothing but that hopeless sense of the transitoriness of life, which precedes, as it survives, all culture and all philosophy. It is only the later dramas that have any ethical tendency, and the change is owing to Confucian and to Buddhist influence.

The value of such a literature will be very differently

* See p. 88.

† For the sole partial exception to this statement, see p. 46.

estimated according as the critic takes or does not take utilitarian views of the subject. If he incline to such views, then certainly the Japanese Muse can say little in her own defence, for she teaches us little or nothing that will either increase our science, or tend to improve our actions. In fact, as already said, she does not consider it her mission to *teach* at all. It is, then, merely as works of art that her productions must be judged; and, for our own part, if we had to express in one word the impression left on our mind by an attentive consideration of them, that one word would be *prettiness.* As in Japanese scenery we miss the awe-inspiring grandeur of the Alps and the vast magnificence of the wide-watered plains of the American continent, but are charmed at each turn by the merry plashing of a mountain torrent, the quaintly painted eaves of some little temple picturesquely perched on a hill-side amid plantations of pines and cryptomerias, or by the view of fantastic islets covered with bamboos and azaleas as we thread our way through the mazes of the inland sea, so do we seem, on turning over the pages of the Japanese poets, to be, as it were, transported to some less substantial world, where the deeper and wider aspects of things are forgotten, and where prettiness and a sort of tender grace are allowed to reign supreme. The Japanese themselves would doubtless dispute this judgment, as containing all too faint praise. But when they tell us* of their verses "making heaven and

* Preface to the "Odes Ancient and Modern." Equally exaggerated praise is to be met with in many other places. It is in the same celebrated preface that occurs the absurd attempt to deck out the simple songs of Japan with the Chinese titles of "metaphorical," "allusive," &c.

earth to tremble, and bringing tears to the eyes of the very demons," we ask, but ask in vain, to be shown any masterpieces that might warrant statements even far less enthusiastic.

It was on a national mind producing a poetry of this complexion that the influence of China was brought to bear. The Japanese were at once led intellectually captive by their more highly gifted neighbours, and even in the poetical domain they first of all endeavoured to make out that their compositions might be distributed into certain Chinese categories, and then, finding this difficult, turned to the composition of actual Chinese verse, an accomplishment which has been cultivated down to the present day with the indifferent success that might have been expected. But to change the native poetry was beyond their power. Its very simplicity saved it. It was open to attack on too few points, and the language and literature which attacked it were, however intrinsically superior, too uncouth, or at least too dissimilar in form, to be capable of even slow assimilation. There are not in the poetical vocabulary of Japan a dozen Chinese words, although the language of business and of common life swarms with them in the degree to which all practical matters have been affected by Chinese influence; neither, until a very late period, can we trace any Chinese or other foreign philosophical ideas in the productions of the Japanese poetical writers.

Thus did the native poetry continue to exist. But its existence gradually became an artificial one. Never wide in scope, and cut off from the living interests which were all bound up with the Chinese civilisation that had found in Japan a new home, there at last remained nothing for the bard to say, except indeed to intone an endless round of frivolous repetitions, and to torture verse into acrostics for the amusement of a degenerate court.

IV.

A few words on what may be termed the externals of the subject under consideration may not come amiss. The Japanese name for "poem" is allied to the word "to sing," and it is the opinion of the native literati that in olden days all poems were sung. This, however, is a matter of conjecture. In the texts themselves there is a remarkable absence of reference to the art of music, and certainly none of the ancient secular tunes have been handed down. All that we know is that the various odes were composed from time to time as occasion might suggest, and then written down and preserved as family relics, for which reason the term "Family collection" is still in use to designate a poet's productions. It was from manuscript family collections of this kind that the "*Mañyefushifu*" and other imperial collections were compiled; for although printing was known in China as early as the time of Alfred the Great, it was scarcely used in Japan before the beginning of the seventeenth century. The poetical tournaments mentioned by European writers for the composition of short odes, on subjects drawn by lot, were not in vogue until the Middle Ages, when real poetry was already defunct, poetastering having taken its place. They therefore call for no mention here.

The manner of representing the lyric dramas is peculiar. The stage, which has remained unaltered in every respect since the beginning of the fifteenth century, when the early dramatists Seami and Otoami acted at Kiyauto before the then Shiyauguñ,* Yoshimasa, is a square wooden room open on all sides but one, and supported on pillars, the side of the square being about eighteen English feet. It is surmounted by a quaint roof somewhat resembling those to be seen on the Japanese Buddhist temples, and is connected with the green-room by a gallery some nine feet wide. Upon this gallery part of the action occasionally takes place. Added on to the back of the square stage is a narrow space where sits the orchestra, consisting of one flute-player, two performers on instruments which, in the absence of a more fitting name, may perhaps be called tambourines, and one beater of the drum, while the chorus, whose number is not fixed, squat on the ground to the right of the spectator. In a line with the chorus, between it and the audience, sits the less important of the two actors † during the greater portion of the piece. The back of the stage, the only side not open to the air, is painted with a pine-tree in accordance with ancient usage, while, equally in conformity to established rules, three small pine-trees are planted

* More commonly called by Europeans the Shogun or Tycoon. At first nothing but military commanders, the Shiyauguñ soon absorbed all real political power, and were practically kings of the country until the revolution of 1868.

† Two was the number of the actors during the golden days of the art. "Nakamitsu," which is a late piece, written when the poetical drama of the Middle Ages was already passing over into the prose play of modern times, contains several characters. It is the Abbot who would sit in the place indicated in the text.

in the court which divides the gallery from the space occupied by the less distinguished portion of the audience. The covered place for the audience, who all sit on the mats according to the immemorial custom of their countrymen, runs round three sides of the stage, the most honourable seats being those which directly face it. Masks are worn by such of the actors as take the parts of females or of supernatural beings, and the dresses are gorgeous in the extreme. Scenery, however, is allowed no place on the lyric stage, though carried to such perfection at the theatres where are acted the more modern plays. A true sense of the fitness of things seems, on this point, to have kept the actors faithful to the old traditions of their art. For on the few occasions, occurring mostly in the later pieces, where this rule is broken through, and an attempt made at scenic effect, the spectator cannot help feeling that the spell is in a manner broken, so completely ideal a performance being only marred by the adoption of any of the adventitious aids of the melodramatic stage.* The same remark applies to the statuesque immobility of the actors, and to the peculiar intonation of the recitative. When once the ear has become used to its loudness, it is by no means unpleasing, while the measured cadences of the chorus are from the very first both soothing and impressive. The music, unfortunately, cannot claim like praise, and the dancing executed by the chief character towards the

* For a different view of this absence of scenery, see Mitford's "Tales of Old Japan," vol. i. p. 164, where an interesting analysis is given of a set of lyric pieces acted before H.R.H. the Duke of Edinburgh, including the "Robe of Feathers," translated below.

close of each piece is tedious and meaningless to the European spectator. The performance occupies a whole day. For although each piece takes, on an average, but one hour to represent, five or six are given in succession, and the intervals between them filled up by the acting of comic scenes.

Down to the time of the late revolution, much ceremony and punctilious etiquette hedged in on every side those who were admitted to the honour of viewing these dramatic performances at the Shiyauguñ's court. Now the doors are open to all alike, but it is still chiefly the old aristocracy who make up the audience; and even they, highly trained as they are in the ancient literature, usually bring with them a book of the play, to enable them to follow with the eye the difficult text, which is rendered still harder of comprehension by the varying tones of the choric chant.

V.

Shall translations from foreign poetry be made in prose or in verse? or, to change the form of the question, shall we reproduce the actual words of the original, or make ourselves the interpreters of its intention? Shall we sacrifice the spirit to the letter, or the letter to the spirit?

This question, this perplexity, is as old as the art of translation, and, by its very nature, admits of no authoritative and satisfactory solution; for different minds will inevitably approach it with contrary prepossessions, so that the debate between the literalists and their adversaries must ever remain an open one. This advantage, at least, is the translator's, to whichever choice his own opinion may incline him, that even if he be thought to err, he must be admitted to have erred in good company,—here, in the field of Oriental translation, more especially. While Sir John Davis contends for the vehicle of verse, Mons. De Rosny prefers prose, and Dr. Legge's practice has varied in his two versions of the same book.* Other names (though of less authority) may be adduced on both sides of the question.

The ideal, presumably, of all translators of poetry would be a version in which the general spirit and the *ipsissima verba* of the original should both be equally preserved. Unfortunately this ideal is scarcely attainable in practice, save in the case of such cognate dialects as English and German or Italian and Spanish. Even when we come to render English verse into French, the difficulty makes itself pressingly felt. How much more so when the two idioms are divided from one another by an interval of a thousand years and by the breadth of the whole globe, as is the case with modern English and classical Japanese!

It would seem to be an illusive idea that any translation from the poetry of an utterly unrelated people *can* be literal (in any fair sense of the word "literal"), however inelegant, however queer-sounding, and however prosaic it may become in the attempt. In the case of the Japanese lyric dramas, a more special

* The "She King," a collection of the most ancient classical poems of China.

reason for a free versified rendering is to be found in the peculiar *soldering* (so to speak) of the style, which has been already touched on, and which makes a literal version not so much difficult as impossible, for the simple reason that there is no logical sense or sentence to be translated, for all that there is to the ear the sweetest poetical sense and music in these vague, unfettered periods, in these

> "Notes with many a winding bout
> Of linkèd sweetness long drawn out
> With wanton heed and giddy cunning."

If such compositions are to be reproduced at all in a European dress, none, probably, would deny that, as the original cannot, by its very nature, be literally transferred to any other tongue, at least the aim should be to do justice, not only to the general sense, but also to the delightful rhythmic melody. The attempt may, indeed, be condemned as rash, howsoever it be made. From another point of view, however, it would be unjustifiable to pass over altogether a branch of Japanese poetry which is worthy of much more attention than it has hitherto received from European scholars; and for this reason there is here given of four of these pieces what, after all possible care has been taken to ensure such accuracy as is alone compatible with the nature of the originals, must still be deemed a paraphrase. With regard to all the other poems composing this volume, a much greater degree of fidelity to the Japanese text has been aimed at, and, it is hoped, attained. The versions claim to be, not paraphrases, but as fairly faithful translations as the widely divergent genius of the English and Japanese tongues and methods of thought will permit, only such originals as proved themselves sufficiently pliable having been allowed to pass muster.

The choice of the poetical form, however, for his versions, by no means terminates the translator's preliminary embarrassments. English, unfortunately — or we should rather say fortunately — differs from Japanese in possessing a whole array of various metres. But to none of these, as has been already seen, does the form of versification adopted by the poets of Japan bear the faintest resemblance. The question is, which English metre will most fitly set forth the spirit of the Oriental originals ?—a question more easily asked than answered. The "parallelism" already referred to as an occasional ornament of Japanese poetry, suggests the use of the unrhymed trochaic measure of "Hiawatha," which seems specially calculated to give such parallel verses their due effect; and it has accordingly been adopted in the version of such of the odes as are most strongly marked by this characteristic. The trochaic metre, however, though comparatively easy to write, is beyond all comparison tedious to read, except when wielded by a master-hand; nor would it properly reproduce the more delicate and varied rhythm of most Japanese classical productions, especially of the ballads and love-songs. It has, therefore, been attempted, by a separate consideration of each individual piece, to determine which form of verse will most aptly render, in each special instance, the spirit and movement of the original, and in many cases a selection has been made from among various translations. On the other hand, the rhythm of the short verse of thirty-one syllables is so peculiar, and so constant, by whatever author it may be handled, that it has been judged best to reproduce it in every instance in the same English form, viz., a four-lined stanza, slight differences of melody being represented by an occasional change in the position of the rhymes.

The whole question, of course, is one of ear, and it must be left to more competent scholars to decide whether the translator's ear has guided him as correctly as the circumstances of the case will allow. To such as would argue, from the absence of rhyme in Japanese poetry, to the necessity of excluding rhyme from an English translation, it may suffice to point out, that English blank verse is, in reality, as different from the Japanese metre as is English rhymed verse, reposing, as it does, on completely different principles; and also that many of the best translators of Western classical poetry, from Dryden downwards, have not hesitated to adopt rhyme, and even to break up the continuous flow of Greek and Latin hexameters, to fit them into the straiter limits of the modern stanza.

NOTE ON THE SPELLING OF JAPANESE PROPER NAMES.

No general agreement as to the best method of translitering Japanese having as yet been arrived at by European students of the language, great confusion still prevails in the Roman spelling of native names of persons and places. Most writers seem to have taken as their standard the modern pronunciation of the portion of the country with which they happened themselves to be most familiar, and to have written down the words, more or less approximately, by ear. Such a plan, which is not without its drawbacks, even in the case of a spoken dialect, is singularly inapplicable to a dead language such as ancient Japanese, which differs as much from the speech of the present day as Latin does from Italian, and whose true pronunciation is not to be ascertained with any certainty. It has, therefore, been thought advisable in the present work to follow a more regular system, suggested by Mr. Satow in vol. vii. part iii. of the "Transactions of the Asiatic Society of Japan," and which consists in simply reproducing in Roman letters each syllable of the original precisely as it is written. It seems almost certain that in ancient times each letter was sounded, though that is no longer the case; thus, *Mañyefushifu* is now pronounced in three syllables, *Manyôshyu.* As a rough general rule, it will be best to give to the consonants their English, and to the vowels their Italian, value. Japanese has, like French, little or no tonic accent; and such native names as are introduced into the translations have, therefore, been accentuated on whatever syllable best suits the metre.

Ballads

FROM THE

"MAÑYEFUSHIFU;"

OR,

"*COLLECTION OF A MYRIAD LEAVES.*"

BALLADS.

The Fisher Boy Urashima.*

'Tis spring, and the mists come stealing
   O'er Suminóye's shore,
And I stand by the seaside musing
   On the days that are no more.

I muse on the old-world story,
   As the boats glide to and fro,
Of the fisher-boy Urashima,
   Who a-fishing lov'd to go;

How he came not back to the village
   Though sev'n suns had risen and set,
But row'd on past the bounds of ocean,
   And the sea-god's daughter met;

How they pledged their faith to each other,
   And came to the Evergreen Land,
And enter'd the sea-god's palace
   So lovingly hand in hand,

* For a literal prose version of this ballad see the second Appendix to Aston's "Grammar of the Japanese Written Language."

C

To dwell for aye in that country,
The ocean-maiden and he,—
The country where youth and beauty
Abide eternally.

But the foolish boy said, "To-morrow
I'll come back with thee to dwell;
But I have a word to my father,
A word to my mother to tell."

The maiden answered, "A casket
I give into thine hand;
And if that thou hopest truly
To come back to the Evergreen Land,

"Then open it not, I charge thee!
Open it not, I beseech!"
So the boy row'd home o'er the billows
To Suminóye's beach.

But where is his native hamlet?
Strange hamlets line the strand.
Where is his mother's cottage?
Strange cots rise on either hand.

"What, in three short years since I left it,"
He cries in his wonder sore,
"Has the home of my childhood vanished?
Is the bamboo fence no more?

"Perchance if I open the casket
  Which the maiden gave to me,
My home and the dear old village
  Will come back as they used to be."

And he lifts the lid, and there rises
  A fleecy, silvery cloud,
That floats off to the Evergreen Country:—
  And the fisher-boy cries aloud;

He waves the sleeve of his tunic,
  He rolls over on the ground,
He dances with fury and horror,
  Running wildly round and round.*

But a sudden chill comes o'er him
  That bleaches his raven hair,
And furrows with hoary wrinkles
  The form erst so young and fair.

His breath grows fainter and fainter,
  Till at last he sinks dead on the shore;
And I gaze on the spot where his cottage
  Once stood, but now stands no more.

(ANON.)

---

* Such frantic demonstrations of grief are very frequently mentioned in the early poetry, and sound strangely in the ears of those who are accustomed to the more than English reserve of the modern Japanese. Possibly, as in Europe, so in Japan, there may have been a real change of character in this respect.

The legend of Urashima is one of the oldest in the language, and traces of it may even be found in the official annals, where it is stated that "in the twenty-first year of the Mikado Iyuuriyaku, the boy Urashima of Midzunoye, in the district of Yosa, in the province of Tañgo, a descendant of the divinity Shimanemi, went to Elysium in a fishing-boat." And again, that "in the second year of Teñchiyau, under the Mikado Go-Zhiyuñwa . . . the boy Urashima returned, and then disappeared, none knew whither." The dates mentioned correspond to A.D. 477 and 825. Urashima's tomb, together with his fishing-line, the casket given him by the maiden, and two stones said to be precious, are still shown at one of the temples in Kanagaha near Yokohama; and by most of even the educated Japanese, the story, thus historically and topographically certified, is accepted as literally true. In the popular version, the "Evergreen Land," visited by Urashima is changed into the Dragon Palace, to which later Japanese myth, coloured by Chinese tradition, has assigned the residence of the sea-god. The word Dragon Palace is in Japanese *ringu*, or, more properly, *rinkiu*, which is likewise the Japanese pronunciation of the name of the islands we call Loochoo, and the Chinese Liu-kiu; and it has been suggested by some, that the Dragon Palace may be but a fanciful name given by some shipwrecked voyager to those sunny southern isles, whose inhabitants still distinguish themselves, even above their Chinese and Japanese neighbours, by their fondness for the dragon as an artistic and architectural adornment. There is one ode in the "*Mañyefushifu*" which would favour this idea, speaking, as it does, of the orange having been first brought to Japan from the "Evergreen Land" lying to the south.

Ballad

COMPOSED ON SEEING A DEAD BODY BY THE ROADSIDE WHEN CROSSING THE ASHIGARA PASS.*

Methinks from the hedge round the garden
His bride the fair hemp had ta'en,
And woven the fleecy raiment
That ne'er he threw off him again.

For toilsome the journey he journeyed
To serve his liege and his lord,†
Till the single belt that encircled him
Was changed to a thrice-wound cord;

And now, methinks, he was faring
Back home to the country-side,
With thoughts all full of his father,
Of his mother, and of his bride.

But here 'mid the eastern mountains,
Where the awful pass climbs their brow,
He halts in his onward journey
And builds him a dwelling low;

And here he lies stark in his garments,
Dishevelled his raven hair,
And ne'er can he tell me his birthplace,
Nor the name that he erst did bear.

(SAKIMARO.)

* One of the passes by which the traveller from Kiyauto may cross the Hakone range to reach the plain of Yedo.

† *i.e.*, the Mikado. The feudal system did not grow up till many centuries later.

The Maiden of Unáhi.*

In Ashinóya village dwelt
  The Maiden of Unáhi,
On whose beauty the next-door neighbours e'en
  Might cast no wondering eye;

For they locked her up as a child of eight,
  When her hair hung loosely still;
And now her tresses were gathered up,
  To float no more at will.†

And the men all yearn'd that her sweet face
  Might once more stand reveal'd,
Who was hid from gaze, as in silken maze
  The chrysalis lies concealed.

And they formed a hedge around the house,
  And, "I'll wed her!" they all did cry;
And the Champion of Chínu he was there,
  And the Champion of Unáhi.

With jealous love these champions twain
  The beauteous girl did woo;

---

* The letters *nahi* are sounded like our English word *nigh*, and therefore form but one syllable to the ear.

† Anciently (and this custom is still followed in some parts of Japan) the hair of female children was cut short at the neck and allowed to hang down loosely till the age of eight. At twelve or thirteen the hair was generally bound up, though this ceremony was also frequently postponed until marriage. At the present day, the methods of doing the hair of female children, of grown-up girls, and of married women vary considerably.

Each had his hand on the hilt of his sword.
  And a full-charged quiver, too,

Was slung o'er the back of each champion fierce,
  And a bow of snow-white wood
Did rest in the sinewy hand of each;
  And the twain defiant stood,

Crying, "An 'twere for her dear sake,
  Nor fire nor flood I'd fear!"
The maiden heard each daring word,
  But spake in her mother's ear:

"Alas! that I, poor country girl,
  Should cause this jealous strife!
An I may not wed the man I love *
  What profits me my life?

"In Hades' realm † I will await
  The issue of the fray."
These secret thoughts, with many a sigh,
  She whisper'd, and pass'd away.

To the champion of Chínu in a dream
  Her face that night was shown;
So he followed the maid to Hades' shade,
  And his rival was left alone;

* Viz., as we gather from another poem by the same author, the Champion of Chínu.

† The Japanese name for Hades is *Yomi*, allied to the word *yoru*, "night." Few particulars are to be gleaned from the old books. Motowori, the great modern apostle of Shiñtau, writes of it as follows:—"*Hades is a land beneath the earth, whither, when they die, go all men, mean and noble, virtuous and wicked, without distinction.*"

Left alone,—too late! too late!
He gapes at the vacant air,
He shouts, and he yells, and gnashes his teeth,
And dances in wild despair.

"But no! I'll not yield!" he fiercely cries,
"I'm as good a man as he!"
And, girding his poniard, he follows after,
To search out his enemy.

The kinsmen then, on either side,
In solemn conclave met,
As a token for ever and evermore
Some monument for to set,

That the story might pass from mouth to mouth
While heav'n and earth shall stand:
So they laid the maiden in the midst,
And the champions on either hand.

And I, when I hear the mournful tale,
I melt into bitter tears,
As though these lovers I never saw
Had been mine own compeers.

(Mushimaro.)

The Grave of the Maiden of Unáhi.

I stand by the grave where they buried
  The Maiden of Unáhi,
Whom of old the rival champions
  Did woo so jealously.

The grave should hand down through the ages
  Her story for evermore,
That men yet unborn might love her,
  And think on the days of yore.

And so beside the causeway
  They piled up the boulders high;
Nor e'er, till the clouds that o'ershadow us
  Shall vanish from the sky,

May the pilgrim along the causeway
  Forget to turn aside,
And mourn o'er the grave of the Maiden;
  And the village folk, beside,

Ne'er cease from their bitter weeping,
  But cluster around her tomb;
And the ages repeat her story,
  And bewail the Maiden's doom.

Till at last e'en I stand gazing
  On the grave where she now lies low,
And muse with unspeakable sadness
  On the old days long ago.

(Sakimaro.)

The existence of the Maiden of Unáhi is not doubted by any of the native authorities, and, as usual, the tomb is there (or said to be there, for the present writer's search after it on the occasion of a somewhat hurried visit to that part of the country was vain) to attest the truth of the tradition. Ashinoya is the name of the village, and Unáhi of the district. The locality is in the province of Setsutsu, between the present treaty-ports of Kaube and Ohosaka. During the Middle Ages the story went on growing, and it may perhaps not be without interest to see the shape it had assumed by the tenth century. A classical story-book dating from which time, and entitled "*Yamato Mono-gatari*," or "Tales of Japan," tells the tale as follows :—

In days of old there dwelt a maiden in the land of Setsutsu, whose hand was sought in marriage by two lovers. One, Mubara by name, was a native of the same country-side; the other, called Chinu, was a native of the land of Idzumi. The two were alike in years, alike in face, in figure and in stature; and whereas the maiden thought to accept the wooing of him that should the more dearly love her, lo! it fell out that they both loved her with the same love. No sooner faded the light of day, than both came to do their courting, and when they sent her gifts, the gifts were quite alike. Of neither could it be said that he excelled the other, and the girl meanwhile felt sick at heart. Had they been men of lukewarm devotion, neither would ever have obtained the maiden's hand; but it was because both of them, day after day and month after month, stood before the cottage-gate and made evident their affection in ten thousand different ways, that the maiden pined with a divided love. Neither lover's gifts were accepted, and yet both would come and stand, bearing in their hands gifts. The maiden had a father and a mother, and they aid to her, "Sad is it for us to have to bear the burden of thine unseemly conduct, in thus carelessly from month to month, and from year to year, causing others to sorrow. If thou wilt accept the one, after a little time the other's love will cease." The maiden made answer, "That likewise was my thought. But the sameness of the love of both has made me altogether sick at heart. Alas! what shall I do?"

Now in olden days the people dwelt in houses raised on platforms built out into the river 'Ikuta. So the girl's father and mother, summoning to their presence the two lovers, spake thus: "Our child is pining with a love divided by the equal ardour of your worships. But to-day we intend, by whatever means, to fix her choice. One of you showeth his devotion by coming hither from a distant home; the other is our neighbour, but his love is boundless. This one and that are alike worthy of our pitying regard." Both the lovers heard these words with respectful joy; and the father and mother continued: "What we have further in our minds to say is this: floating on our river is a water-bird. Draw your bows at it; and to him that shall strike it, will we have the honour to present our daughter." "Well thought!" replied the lovers twain; and drawing their bows at the same instant, one struck the bird in the head and the other in the tail, so that neither could claim to be the better marksman. Sick with love, the maiden cried out—

> "*Enough, enough! yon swiftly flowing wave*
> *Shall free my soul from her long anxious strife:*
> *Men call fair Settsu's stream the stream of life,*
> *But in that stream shall be the maiden's grave!*" *

and, with these words, let herself fall down into the river from the platform that overlooked it.

While the father and mother, frantic with grief, were raving and shouting, the two lovers plunged together into the stream. One caught hold of the maiden's foot and the other of her hand, and the three sank together and perished in the flood. Terrible was the grief of the girl's father and mother, as, amid tears and lamentations, they lifted her body out of the water and prepared to give it burial. The parents of the two lovers likewise came to the spot, and dug for their sons, graves beside the grave of the maiden. But the father and mother of him that dwelt in the same country-side raised an outcry, saying, "That he who belongs to the same land should be buried in the same place is just. But how shall it be lawful for an alien to desecrate our soil?" So the parents of him that dwelt in Idzumi laded a junk with Idzumi earth, in which, having brought it to the spot, they laid their son: and to this day the maiden's grave stands there in the middle, and the graves of her lovers on either side. Paintings, too, of all these scenes of bygone days have been presented to the former Empress,† and, moved by the pictures, many persons have composed

*** In this stanza the phonetic spelling Settsu has been adopted for the sake of the metre.**

† Probably the consort of the Mikado Uda, who died A.D. 931.

stanzas of poetry, putting themselves in the place of one or other of the three persons of the story. . . . (Here follow a number of thirty-one-syllable stanzas that are not worth the trouble of translating; and the tale then proceeds thus:) Ceremonial garments, trousers, a hat, and a sash were placed in a large hollow bamboo-cane, and buried with the one (i.e., the native of Unáhi), together with a bow, a quiver and a long sword. But the father and mother of the other must have been silly folks, for they prepared nothing in like manner. The "Maiden's Grave" is the name by which the grave is called.

A certain wayfarer, who once passed the night in the neighbourhood of the grave, startled by the sound of fighting, sent his retainers to inquire into the cause thereof. They returned saying that they could hear nothing. But the wayfarer kept pondering on the strange story, and at last fell asleep. Then there rose up before him a blood-stained man, who, kneeling at his side, spake thus: "I am sorely harassed by the persecutions of an enemy, and entreat thee to condescend to lend me thy sword that I may be revenged on my tormentor." The request filled the wayfarer with alarm; nevertheless, he lent his sword, and, shortly awaking, imagined it to have been but a dream; yet in very truth the sword was missing; and, as he listened attentively, his ear caught the same terrific sound of fighting that had struck it at first. But a brief time elapsed before the spectre reappeared, and exclaimed exultingly: "By thine honourable assistance have I slain the foe that had oppressed me during these many years. From henceforward I will for ever watch over thy safety." He then told the tale from the beginning to the wayfarer, who, notwithstanding that the whole matter seemed to him to have an ugly look, would have inquired more particularly into the rights of so strange a story. But at that moment day began to dawn, and he found himself alone. The next morning, from the foot of the grave a stream of blood was seen to flow; and the sword also was blood-stained. The tale seems a most uncomfortable one; but I tell it as it was told to me.

The Maiden of Katsushika.

Where in the far-off eastern land
  The cock first crows at dawn,
The people still hand down a tale
  Of days long dead and gone.

They tell of Katsushíka's maid,
  Whose sash of country blue
Bound but a frock of home-spun hemp,
  And kirtle coarse to view;

Whose feet no shoe had e'er confined,
  Nor comb passed through her hair;
Yet all the queens in damask robes
  Might nevermore compare

With this dear child, who smiling stood,
  A flow'ret of the spring,—
In beauty perfect and complete,
  Like to the full moon's ring.

And, as the summer moths that fly
  Towards the flame so bright,
Or as the boats that seek the port
  When fall the shades of night,

So came the suitors; but she said:
  "Why take me for your wife?
Full well I know my humble lot,
  I know how short my life." *

* The original of this stanza is obscure, and the native commentators have no satisfactory interpretation to offer.

So where the dashing billows beat
  On the loud-sounding shore,
Hath Katsushíka's tender maid
  Her home for evermore.

Yes! 'tis a tale of days long past;
  But, list'ning to the lay,
It seems as I had gazed upon
  Her face but yesterday.

(ANON.)

To the slight, but undoubtedly very ancient, tradition preserved in the foregoing ballad, there is nothing to add from any authentic source. Popular fancy, however, has been busy filling up the gaps, and introduces a cruel stepmother, who, untouched by the piety of the maiden in drawing water for her every day from the only well whose water she cares to drink, is so angry with her for, by her radiant beauty, attracting suitors to the house, that the poor girl ends by drowning herself, upon which the neighbours declare her to be a goddess, and erect a temple in her honour. Both the temple and the well are still among the show-places in the environs of Yedo.

The Beggar's Complaint.*

The heaven and earth they call so great,
  For me are mickle small;
The sun and moon they call so bright,
  For me ne'er shine at all.

---

* In the original the title is "The Beggar's Dialogue," there being two poems, of which that here translated is the second. The first one, which is put into the mouth of an unmarried beggar, who takes a cheerier view of poverty, is not so well fitted for translation into English.

Are all men sad, or only I ?
   And what have I obtained,—
What good the gift of mortal life,
   That prize so rarely gained,*

If naught my chilly back protects
   But one thin grass-cloth coat,
In tatters hanging like the weeds
   That on the billows float,—

If here in smoke-stained, darksome hut,
   Upon the bare cold ground,
I make my wretched bed of straw,
   And hear the mournful sound,—

Hear how mine agèd parents groan,
   And wife and children cry,
Father and mother, children, wife,
   Huddling in misery,—

If in the rice-pan, nigh forgot,
   The spider hangs its nest,†
And from the hearth no smoke goes up
   Where all is so unblest ?

And now, to make our wail more deep,
   That saying is proved true
Of "snipping what was short before :"—
   Here comes to claim his due

* Because, according to the Buddhist doctrine of perpetually recurring births, it is at any given time more probable that the individual will come into the world in the shape of one of the lower animals.

† A literal translation of the Japanese idiom.

The village provost, stick in hand,
He's shouting at the door;—
And can such pain and grief be all
Existence has in store?

Stanza.

Shame and despair are mine from day to day;
But, being no bird, I cannot fly away.
(ANON.)

A Frontier Soldier's Regrets on Leaving Home.*

When I left to keep guard on the frontier
(For such was the monarch's decree),
My mother, with skirt uplifted,†
Drew near and fondled me;

And my father, the hot tears streaming
His snow-white beard adown,

---

* The "Frontiers" in the early part of the eighth century of our era were, north, at a line drawn roughly across the main island of Japan at latitude 38°, and separating the Japanese proper from the aboriginal Ainos, and, south, the island of Kinshiu. Neither Yezo nor Loochoo had as yet been added to the empire. Troops sent to the Corea (see p. 79) were likewise said to be doing "frontier service." The mention of embarking at Naniha (near the site of the modern treaty-port of Ohosaka) shows that it was on duty in the south or west that the author of this piece was sent.

† The Japanese commentators do not help us much towards a comprehension of this curious passage (lit. took up in her fingers the lower part of her skirt, and stroked"). One of them supposes that she lifted up her skirt in order to be better able to walk towards her son and caress him.

Besought me to tarry, crying:
  "Alas! when thou art gone,

"When thou leav'st our gate in the morning,
  No other sons have I,
And mine eyes will long to behold thee
  As the weary years roll by;

"So tarry but one day longer,
  And let me find some relief
In speaking and hearing thee speak to me!"
  So wail'd the old man in his grief.

And on either side came pressing
  My wife and my children dear,
Flutt'ring like birds, and with garments
  Besprinkled with many a tear;

And clasp'd my hands, and would stay me,
  For 'twas so hard to part;
But mine awe of the sovereign edict
  Constrained my loving heart.

I went; yet each time the pathway
  O'er a pass through the mountains did wind,
I'd turn me round—ah! so lovingly!—
  And ten thousand times gaze behind.

But farther still, and still farther,
  Past many a land I did roam,
And my thoughts were all thoughts of sadness,
  All loving, sad thoughts of home:—

Till I came to the shores of Sumi,
Where the sovereign gods * I prayed,
With off'rings so humbly offered,—
And this the prayer that I made :—

"Being mortal, I know not how many
The days of my life may be;
And now the perilous pathway
That leads o'er the plain of the sea,

"Past unknown islands will bear me:
But grant that while I am gone
No hurt may touch father or mother,
Or the wife now left all alone!"

Yes, such was my prayer to the sea-gods;
And now the unnumber'd oars,†
And the ship and the seamen to bear me
From breezy Nanĩha's shores

Are there at the mouth of the river:—
Oh! tell the dear ones at home,
That I'm off as the day is breaking
To row o'er the ocean foam.‡

(ANON.)

* Their names are Sokodzutsuwo, Nakadzutsuwo, and Uhadzutsuwo, and together they rule the sea. To them is often associated the semi-fabulous Empress Zhiñgou, who is said to have conquered the Corea in the third century of our era.

† In the earliest Japanese literature there is but little mention made of sailing, and even so late as the tenth century the oar would seem to have remained the chief means of propulsion at sea.

‡ To whom this request is made does not appear.

Love Songs

FROM THE

"MAÑYEFUSHIFU;"

OR,

"*COLLECTION OF A MYRIAD LEAVES.*"

LOVE SONGS.

—o—

Song

COMPOSED BY THE COMMANDER-IN-CHIEF ON BEHOLDING THE MOUNTAINS, WHEN THE MIKADO MADE A PROGRESS TO THE DISTRICT OF AYA IN THE PROVINCE OF SANUKI.*

The long spring day is o'er, and dark despond
  My heart invades, and lets the tears flow down,
As all alone I stand, when from beyond
  The mount our heav'n-sent monarch's throne doth
      crown

There breathes the twilight wind and turns my sleeve.
  Ah, gentle breeze! to turn, home to return,
Is all my prayer; I cannot cease to grieve
  On this long toilsome road; I burn, I burn!

* This commander-in-chief's name is not to be ascertained. The Mikado mentioned would seem to be Zhiyomei, who, according to the history, made a progress to the hot baths of Aya in the winter of A.D. 639–640. Sanuki is one of the four provinces forming the island of Shikoku, which lies between the Inland Sea and the Pacific Ocean. Tsunu is a village on the coast. Salt-burning, as it is called, is still a considerable industry in the maritime districts of Japan.

Yes! the poor heart I used to think so brave
Is all afire, though none the flame may see,
Like to the salt-kilns there by Tsunu's wave,
Where toil the fisher-maidens wearily.

(ANON.)

Lines

SENT TO HIS MISTRESS WHEN THE POET WAS LEAVING THE PROVINCE OF IHAMI* TO GO UPON IMPERIAL SERVICE TO THE CAPITAL.

Tsunu's shore, Ihámi's brine,
To all other eyes but mine
Seem, perchance, a lifeless mere,
And sands that ne'er the sailor cheer.
Ah, well-a-day! no ports we boast,
And dead the sea that bathes our coast;
But yet I trow the wingèd breeze
Sweeping at morn across our seas,
And the waves at eventide
From the depths of ocean wide,
Onward to Watadzu bear
The deep-green seaweed, rich and fair;
And like that seaweed, gently swaying,
Wingèd breeze and waves obeying,
So thy heart hath swayed and bent
And crowned my love with thy consent.

---

* On the north-west coast of the main island of Japan. There is no rise and fall of the tide in this portion of the Japan Sea,—a fact all the more remarkable, as the tides are particularly strong on the opposite shores of the Corea. Tsunu and Watadzu are the names of villages, the former not to be confounded with Tsunu in Sanuki. It was at Tsunu that the poet's mistress dwelt.

But, dear heart! I must away,
As fades the dew when shines the day;
Nor aught my backward looks avail,
Myriad times cast down the vale
From each turn the winding road
Takes upward; for thy dear abode
Farther still and farther lies,
And hills on hills between us rise.
Ah! bend ye down, ye cruel peaks,
That the gate my fancy seeks,
Where sits my pensive love alone,
To mine eyes again be shown!

(HITOMARO.)

Love is Pain.

'Twas said of old, and still the ages say,
" The lover's path is full of doubt and woe."
Of me they spake: I know not, nor can know,
If she I sigh for will my love repay.
My head sinks on my breast; with bitter strife
My heart is torn, and grief she cannot see.
All unavailing is this agony
To help the love that has become my life.

(ANON.)

No Tidings.

The year has come, the year has gone again,
And still no tidings of mine absent love:
Through the long days of spring all heaven above
And earth beneath re-echo with my pain.

In dark cocoon my mother's silkworms dwell;
Like them, a captive, through the livelong day
Alone I sit and sigh my soul away,
For ne'er to any I my love may tell.

Like to the *pine*-trees I must stand and *pine*,*
While downward slanting fall the shades of night,
Till my long sleeve of purest snowy white
With showers of tears is steeped in bitter brine.

(ANON.)

Love is All.

WHERE in spring the sweetest flowers
Fill Mount Kaminábi's bowers,
Where in autumn, dyed with red,
Each ancient maple rears its head,
And Aska's † flood, with sedges lin'd,
As a belt the mound doth bind:—
There see my heart,—a reed that sways,
Nor aught but love's swift stream obeys,
And now, if, like the dew, dear maid,
Life must fade, then let it fade:
My secret love is not in vain,
For thou lov'st me back again.‡

(ANON.)

---

* The play in the original is on the word *matsu*, which has the double signification of "a pine-tree" and "to wait."

† Thus pronounced, but properly written Asuka.

‡ Though no formal comparison is expressed, the allusions to the blossoms, to the ruddy tint, and to the girdle, are meant to apply to the poet's mistress as well as to the scenery of Kaminábi. These suggestions, as it were from without, are much sought after by the poets of Japan.

Homeward.

From Kaminábi's crest
The clouds descending pour in sheeted rain,
And, 'midst the gloom, the wind sighs o'er the
plain :—
Oh ! he that sadly press'd,
Leaving my loving side, alone to roam
Magámi's des'late moor, has he reach'd home ?

(ANON.)

The Maiden and her Dog.

As the bold huntsman on some mountain path
Waits for the stag he hopes may pass that way,
So wait I for my love both night and day :
Then bark not at him, as thou fear'st my wrath !

(ANON.)

Secret Love.

If as my spirit yearns for thine
Thine yearns for me, why thus delay ?
And yet, what answer might be mine
If, pausing on her way,
Some gossip bade me tell
Whence the deep sighs that from my bosom
swell ?

And thy dear name my lips should pass,
My blushes would our loves declare ;

No, no! I'll say my longing was
To see the moon appear
O'er yonder darkling hill;
Yet 'tis on thee mine eyes would gaze their fill!

(ANON.)

He comes not.*

He comes not! 'tis in vain I wait;
The crane's wild cry strikes on mine ear,
The tempest howls, the hour is late,
Dark is the raven night and drear:
And, as I thus stand sighing,
The snowflakes round me flying
Light on my sleeve, and freeze it crisp and clear.

Sure 'tis too late! he cannot come;
Yet trust I still that we may meet,
As sailors gaily rowing home
Trust in their ship so safe and fleet.
Though waking hours conceal him,
Oh! may my dreams reveal him,
Filling the long, long night with converse sweet!

(ANON.)

The Omen.

[The reference in this song is to an old superstition. It used to be supposed that the chance words caught from the mouths of passers-by, would solve any doubt or question to which it might

* The translation is here made, not from the standard text, but from a slightly varying one quoted in the "*Riyakuge*" commentary.

otherwise be impossible to obtain an answer. This was called the *yufu-ura*, or "evening divination," on account of its being practised in the evening. It has been found impossible in this instance to follow the original very closely.]

Yes! 'twas the hour when all my hopes
  Seemed idle as the dews that shake
And tremble in their lotus-cups
    By deep Tsurúgi's lake,—
    'Twas then the omen said:
"Fear not! he'll come his own dear love to wed."

What though my mother bids me flee
  Thy fond embrace? No heed I take;
As pure, as deep my love for thee
    As Kiyosúmi's lake.
    One thought fills all my heart:
When wilt thou come no more again to part?

(ANON.)

Rain and Snow.

For ever on Mikáne's crest,
  That soars so far away,
The rain it rains in ceaseless sheets,
  The snow it snows all day.

And ceaseless as the rain and snow
  That fall from heaven above,
So ceaselessly, since first we met,
  I love my darling love.

(ANON.)

Parted by the Stream.

Here on one side of the stream I stand,
And gaze on my love on the other strand.
  Oh! not to be with her, what sadness!
  Oh! not to be with her, what madness!

If but a red-lacquered skiff were mine,
With paddles strewn over with pearls so fine,
  Then would I pass the river,
  And dwell with my love for ever!

(ANON.)

He and She.

He. To Hatsúse's vale I'm come,
To woo thee, darling, in thy home
But the rain rains down apace,
And the snow veils ev'ry place,
And now the pheasant 'gins to cry,
And the cock crows to the sky:
Now flees the night, the night hath fled,
Let me in to share thy bed!

She. To Hatsúse's vale thou'rt come,
To woo me, darling, in my home:
But my mother sleeps hard by,
And my father near doth lie;
Should I but rise, I'll wake her ear;
Should I go out, then he will hear:
The night hath fled! it may not be,
For our love's a mystery!

(ANON.)

Husband and Wife.

Wife. While other women's husbands ride
  Along the road in proud array,
My husband up the rough hillside
  On foot must wend his weary way.

The grievous sight with bitter pain
  My bosom fills, and many a tear
Steals down my cheek, and I would fain
  Do ought to help my husband dear.

Come! take the mirror and the veil,
  My mother's parting gifts to me;
In barter they must sure avail
  To buy an horse to carry thee!

Husband. An I should purchase me an horse,
  Must not my wife still sadly walk?
No, no! though stony is our course,
  We'll trudge along and sweetly talk.

(ANON.)

The Pearls.*

Oh! he my prince, that left my side
  O'er the twain Lover Hills † to roam,

---

* For the reference in this song to the "evening horoscope," see p. 59.

† Mount Lover and Mount Lady-love (Se-yama and Imo-yama), in the province of Yamato. Between them ran the rapid Yoshino-gaha, which has ended by sweeping away the Lover's Mount,—at least so the translator was told by the ferryman at the river in the summer of 1876; and

Saying that in far Kíshiu's tide
He'd hunt for pearls to bring them home,

When will he come? With trembling hope
I hie me to the busy street
To ask the evening horoscope,
That straightway thus gives answer meet—

"The lover dear, my pretty girl,
For whom thou waitest, comes not yet,
Because he's seeking ev'ry pearl
Where out at sea the billows fret.

"He comes not yet, my pretty girl!
Because among the riplets clear
He's seeking, finding ev'ry pearl;
'Tis that delays thy lover dear.

"Two days at least must come and go,
Sev'n days at most will bring him back;
'Twas he himself that told me so:
Then cease fair maid, to cry Alack!"

(ANON.)

Lines

COMPOSED ON BEHOLDING AN UNACCOMPANIED DAMSEL CROSSING THE GREAT BRIDGE OF KAHAUCHI.

Across the bridge, with scarlet lacquer glowing,
That o'er the Katashíha's stream is laid,

---

certainly from the boat there was but one mountain to be seen in the direction indicated. Perhaps there was never more than one, save in the brains of the Japanese poets, who are very fond of playing with these romantic names.

All trippingly a tender girl is going,
  In bodice blue and crimson skirt arrayed.
None to escort her: would that I were knowing
  Whether alone she sleeps on virgin bed,
Or if some spouse has won her by his wooing:—
  Tell me her house! I'll ask the pretty maid!

(ANON.)

Evening.

From the loud wave-wash'd shore
  Wend I my way,
Hast'ning o'er many a flow'r,
  At close of day,—
On past Kusáka's crest,
  Onward to thee,
Sweet as the loveliest
  Flower of the lea!

(ANON.)

A note to the original says: "The name of the composer of the above song is not given because he was of obscure rank," a reason which will sound strange to European ears. See, however, the Introduction, p. 17.]

A Maiden's Lament.

Full oft he sware, with accents true and tender,
  "Though years roll by, my love shall ne'er wax old!"
And so to him my heart I did surrender,
  Clear as a mirror of pure burnish'd gold;

And from that day, unlike the seaweed bending
To ev'ry wave raised by the autumn gust,
Firm stood my heart, on him alone depending,
As the bold seaman in his ship doth trust.

Is it some cruel god that hath bereft me?
Or hath some mortal stol'n away his heart?
No word, no letter since the day he left me,
Nor more he cometh, ne'er again to part!

In vain I weep, in helpless, hopeless sorrow,
From earliest morn until the close of day;
In vain, till radiant dawn brings back the morrow,
I sigh the weary, weary nights away.

No need to tell how young I am and slender,—
A little maid that in thy palm could lie:
Still for some message comforting and tender
I pace the room in sad expectancy.

(The Lady Sakanouhe.)

Song

COMPOSED ON ASCENDING MOUNT MIKASA.*

Oft in the misty spring
The vapours roll o'er Mount Mikasa's crest,
While, pausing not to rest,
The birds each morn with plaintive note do sing.

---

* In the province of Yamato, close to Nara, the ancient capital.

Like to the mists of spring
My heart is rent; for, like the song of birds,
Still all unanswer'd ring
The tender accents of my passionate words.
I call her ev'ry day
Till daylight fades away;
I call her ev'ry night
Till dawn restores the light;—
But my fond pray'rs are all too weak to bring
My darling back to sight.

(AKAHITO.)

Song

ASKING FOR PEARLS TO SEND HOME TO NARA.

They tell me that the fisher-girls
Who steer their course o'er Susu's* brine,
Dive 'neath the waves and bring up pearls :—
Oh! that five hundred pearls were mine!

Forlorn upon our marriage-bed,
My wife, my darling sweet and true,
Must lay her solitary head
Since the sad hour I bade adieu.

No more, methinks, when shines the dawn,
She combs her dark dishevell'd hair:

* A place in the province of Noto, the little peninsula that juts out into the Japan Sea on the north-west coast.

She counts the months since I am gone,
She counts the days with many a tear.

If but a string of pearls were mine,
I'd please her with them, and I'd say,
"With flags and orange-blossoms * twine
Them in a wreath on summer's day."
(YAKAMOCHI.)

The Flowers of my Garden.

Sent by the sov'reign lord to sway
The farthest lands that own his might,
To Koshi's † wilds I came away,
Where stretch the snows all wintry white.

And now five years are past and gone,
And still I sleep on widowed bed,
Nor loose my belt, nor, being thus lone,
May pillow on thine arm my head.

But as a solace for my heart,
Before my dwelling, pinks I sow,
And lilies small, with gard'ner's art
Ta'en from the summer moor below;

---

* Literally, the *tachibana* (*citrus mandarinus*), one of the orange tribe.
† The most northern province of the empire, on the Aino border.

And never can I leave the house
And see them flow'ring, but I think
On when I'll see my lily spouse,
My spouse as fair as any pink.

Sweet dreams of love! ah! came ye not
The anguish of mine heart to stay,
In this remote and savage spot
I could not live one single day.

(Yakamochi.)

Elegies

FROM THE

'MAÑYEFUSHIFU;"

OR,

"COLLECTION OF A MYRIAD LEAVES."

ELEGIES.

Elegy on the Death of the Mikado Teñji.*

BY ONE OF HIS LADIES.

Alas! poor mortal maid! unfit to hold
High converse with the glorious gods above,†
Each morn that breaks still finds me unconsoled,
Each hour still hears me sighing for my love.

Wert thou a precious stone, I'd clasp thee tight
Around mine arm; wert thou a silken dress,
I'd ne'er discard thee either day or night:—
Last night, sweet love! I dreamt I saw thy face.

(ANON.)

Elegy on the Death of Prince Hinami.

[This prince died A.D. 689 in the twenty-second year of his age. His father, Teñmu, who had died three years previously, had been temporarily succeeded during the statutory years of mourning and

---

* Died A.D. 671. This piece has been translated by Mons. Léon de Rosny in his "Anthologie Japonaise."

† Viz., with the departed and deified Mikado.

the troublous times that ensued by his consort, the Empress Jitou, from whom the throne was to have passed to Prince Hinami as soon as circumstances would permit of the ceremony of his accession.

The first strophe of the elegy deals with the fabulous early history, relating the appointment by a divine council of Ninigi-no-Mikoto as first emperor of the dynasty of the gods in Japan. From him Prince Hinami was descended, and his death is, therefore, in the second strophe, figured as a flight back to heaven, his ancestral home, motived by the inutility of his presence in a world where his mother reigned supreme. The third strophe expresses the grief of the nation, and paints the loneliness of the tomb at Mayumi, which is represented by the poet as a palace where the Prince dwells in solitude and silence. The closing lines refer to the watchers by the tomb, who are removed after a certain time.]

I.

When began the earth and heaven,
By the banks of heaven's river *
All the mighty gods assembled,
All the mighty gods held council,
Thousand myriads held high council;
And (for that her sov'reign grandeur
The great goddess of the day-star
Rul'd th' ethereal realms of heaven)
Downward through the many-pilèd
Welkin did they waft her grandson,
Bidding him, till earth and heaven,
Waxing old, should fall together,
O'er the middle land of Reed-plains,
O'er the land of waving Rice-fields,†
Spread abroad his power imperial.

* The Milky Way.
† Old poetical names for Japan.

II.

But not his Kiyómi's palace:
'Tis his sov'reign's, her's the empire;
And the sun's divine descendant,
Ever soaring, passeth upward
Through the heav'n's high rocky portals.

III.

Why, dear prince, oh! why desert us?
Did not all beneath the heaven,
All that dwell in earth's four quarters,
Pant, with eye and heart uplifted,
As for heav'n-sent rain in summer,
For thy rule of flow'ry fragrance,
For thy plenilune of empire?
Now on lone Mayúmi's hillock,
Firm on everlasting columns,
Pilest thou a lofty palace,
Whence no more, when day is breaking,
Sound thine edicts awe-compelling.
Day to day is swiftly gather'd,
Moon to moon, till e'en thy faithful
Servants from thy palace vanish.

(HITOMARO.)

On the Death of the Poet's Mistress.

How fondly did I yearn to gaze
(For was not there the dear abode
Of her whose love lit up my days ?)
On Karu's often-trodden road.*

But should I wander in and out
Morning and evening ceaselessly,
Our loves were quickly noised about,
For eyes enough were there to see.

So trusting that, as tendrils part
To meet again, so we might meet,
As in deep rocky gorge my heart,
Unseen, unknown, in secret beat.

But like the sun at close of day,
And as behind a cloud the moon,
So passed my gentle love away,
An autumn leaf ta'en all too soon.

When came the fatal messenger,
I knew not what to say or do :—
But who might sit and simply hear ?
Rather, methought, of all my woe,

---

* Karu's Road seems to have been the name of the village. It was in the province of Yamato, not far from the capital.

Haply one thousandth part might find
Relief if my due feet once more,
Where she so often trod, should wind
Through Karu's streets, and past her door.

But mute that voice, nor all the crowd
Could show her like or soothe my care;
So, calling her dear name aloud,
I waved my sleeve in blank despair.

(HITOMARO.)

Lines

SUPPOSED TO HAVE BEEN WRITTEN ON THE OCCASION OF THE DEATH OF THE PRINCE OF MINO (DIED A.D. 708), FATHER OF PRINCE TACHIBANA-NO-MOROYE, COMPILER OF THE "MAÑYEFUSHIFU."

O ye steeds the Prince of Mino
Stabled in his western stables!
O ye steeds the Prince of Mino
Stabled in his eastern stables!
Is it for your food ye whinny?
Then the fodder I will bring you.
Is it for your drink ye whinny?
Then the water I will bring you.
Wherefore neigh the milk-white chargers?

Ah! methinks these steeds have bosoms,
For their voice is chang'd and sadden'd.

(ANON.)

Elegy on the Poet's Young Son Furubi.

Sev'n * are the treasures mortals most do prize,
But I regard them not:
One only jewel could delight mine eyes,—
The child that I begot.

My darling boy, who with the morning sun
Began his joyous day;
Nor ever left me, but with childlike fun
Would make me help him play;

Who'd take my hand when eve its shadows spread,
Saying, "I'm sleepy grown;
'Twixt thee and mother I would lay my head:
Oh! leave me not alone!"

Then, with his pretty prattle in mine ears,
I'd lie awake and scan
The good and evil of the coming years,
And see the child a man.

And, as the seaman trusts his bark, I'd trust
That nought could harm the boy:
Alas! I wist not that the whirling gust
Would shipwreck all my joy!

---

* Viz., gold, silver, emeralds, crystals, rubies, amber (or coral or the diamond), and agate.

Then with despairing, helpless hands I grasp'd
The sacred mirror's sphere; *
And round my shoulder I my garments clasp'd,
And pray'd with many a tear:

"'Tis yours, great gods, that dwell in heav'n on high,
Great gods of earth! 'tis yours
To heed or heed not, a poor father's cry,
Who worships and implores!"

Alas! vain pray'rs, that more no more avail!
He languish'd day by day,
Till e'en his infant speech began to fail,
And life soon ebb'd away.

Stagg'ring with grief I strike my sobbing breast,
And wildly dance and groan:
Ah! such is life! the child that I caress'd
Far from mine arms hath flown!

---

* The part played by the mirror in the devotions of the Japanese is carried back by them to a tale in their mythology which relates the disappearance into a cavern of the Sun-goddess Amaterasu, and the manner in which she was enticed forth by being led to believe that her reflection in a mirror that was shown to her was another deity more lovely than herself. The tying up of the wide sleeve (originally by some creeping plant, and later by a riband), which is still commonly practised by the lower classes when engaged in any manual labour, was also naturally adopted by the priests when making their offerings of fruits, &c., and thus passed into a sign of devotion. In this place may also be mentioned the *nusa*,—offerings of hemp, a plant always looked upon as one of the most precious of the productions of the soil, and presented to the gods as such, or used in the ceremony of purification (see p. 103). In modern times, worthless paper has been substituted for the precious hemp, and the meaning of the ceremony entirely lost sight of, some of the common people even supposed that the gods come down and take up their residence in the strips of paper.

Short Stanza on the Same Occasion.

So young, so young! he cannot know the way:
On Hades' porter * I'll a bribe bestow,
That on his shoulders the dear infant may
Be safely carried to the realms below.
(*Attributed to* OKURA.)

Elegy on the Poet's Wife.

The gulls that twitter on the rush-grown shore
When fall the shades of night,
That o'er the waves in loving pairs do soar
When shines the morning light,—
'Tis said e'en these poor birds delight
To nestle each beneath his darling's wing
That, gently fluttering,
Through the dark hours wards off the hoar-frost's might.

Like to the stream that finds
The downward path it never may retrace,
Like to the shapeless winds,
Poor mortals pass away without a trace:
So she I love has left her place,
And, in a corner of my widowed couch,
Wrapp'd in the robe she wove me, I must crouch
Far from her fond embrace.
(NIBI.)

---

* The reference is a Buddhist one. In a Sutra entitled "*Zhifuwau kiyau*" details are given of several infernal attendants.

Elegy on Yuki-no-Murazhi Ihemaro,

WHO DIED AT THE ISLAND OF IKI ON HIS WAY TO THE COREA.

[Of this personage nothing further is known. The word Kara in the poem signifies the Corea, although in modern Japanese it is exclusively used to designate China. From the most ancient times down to the year 1876, when the pretension was formally renounced, the Mikados laid claim to the possession of the Corea, —a claim which was substantiated by two conquests, one by the Empress Zhiñgou in the beginning of the third century of our era, the other by the armies of Hideyoshi, the Napoleon of Japan, who practically ruled the country during the latter part of the sixteenth century. It must, however, be admitted that the warrior-empress is at most but a semi-historical character, and that, whatever may be the truth as to the alleged early conquest of the Corea by the Japanese, the latter were undoubtedly led captive by the arts and letters of their more cultivated neighbours.]

Sent by the sov'reign monarch to hold sway
O'er Kara's land, he left his native soil;
But ye, his kinsmen, ne'er the gods did pray,
Or else, perchance, the mats ye did defile.*

"In autumn," spake he, "I will come again,
"Dear mother!" But that autumn is forgot;
And days roll by, and moons do wax and wane,
And still they watch, and still he cometh not.

---

* Reference is here made to the custom, not yet extinct, of leaving untouched during a certain time the apartment recently occupied by one who has started on a journey. The idea is that to sweep the mats at once would be, as it were, to wipe him out of remembrance. On the second day, at earliest, the room is cleaned, and food for the absent one brought in at the accustomed hours.

For he ne'er lighted on that distant shore,
Though far he sailed from fair Yamáto's * lea;
But on this cragged rock for evermore
He dwells among the islands of the sea.

(ANON.)

Elegy on the Death of the Corean Nun Riguwañ.

[A note appended to the original poem tells us that Riguwañ, desirous of placing herself under the beneficent sway of the Japanese Emperor, crossed over in the year 714, and for the space of one-and-twenty years sojourned in the house of the Prime Minister Ohotomo. She died in 735 while the Minister and his wife were away at the mineral baths of Arima, a mountain retreat not far from the present port of Kaube. The daughter of the house, Sakanouhe, was alone present at her death and interment, and afterwards sent the following elegy to her mother at Arima. During the sixth, seventh, and eighth centuries there was a very considerable immigration from the Corea into Japan. Artisans and teachers of every description, and even monks and nuns, flocked to what was then a new country.]

Oftimes in far Corea didst thou hear
Of our Cipango as a goodly land;
And so, to parents and to brethren dear
Bidding adieu, thou sailed'st to the strand

---

* Yamato, though properly the particular designation of one of the central provinces, is often used as a name for the whole of Japan. Nara, the ancient capital, is situated in Yamato, and most of the older temporary capitals were within its limits.

Of these domains that own th' imperial pow'r,
Where glitt'ring palaces unnumber'd rise ;
Yet such might please thee not, nor many a bow'r
Where village homesteads greet the pilgrim's eyes :

But in this spot, at Sahoyáma's * base,
Some secret influence bade thee find thy rest,—
Bade seek us out with loving eagerness,
As seeks the weeping infant for the breast.

And here with aliens thou didst choose to dwell,
Year in, year out, in deepest sympathy ;
And here thou builtest thee an holy cell ;
And so the peaceful years went gliding by.

But ah ! what living thing mote yet avoid
Death's dreary summons ?—And thine hour did sound
When all the friends on whom thine heart relied
Slept on strange pillows on the mossy ground.†

So, while the morn lit up Kasúga's crest,
O'er Sahogáha's flood thy corse they bore,
To fill a tomb upon yon mountain's breast,
And dwell in darkness drear for evermore.

No words, alas ! nor efforts can avail :
Nought can I do, poor solitary child !

---

* A mountain in the province of Yamato. The river Sahogáha, mentioned a little farther on, runs past its base.

† This line is an adaptation of the Japanese term *Kusa-makura*, literally "a pillow of herbs," itself the "pillow-word" for the word *journey*.

Nought can I do but make my bitter wail,
And pace the room with cries and gestures wild,

Ceaselessly weeping, till my snowy sleeve
Is wet with tears. Who knows? Perchance again
Wafted they're borne upon the sighs I heave
On 'Arima's far distant heights to rain.

(SAKANOUHE.)

Miscellaneous Poems

FROM THE

"MAÑYEFUSHIFU;"

OR,

"COLLECTION OF A MYRIAD LEAVES."

MISCELLANEOUS POEMS.

Lines

COMPOSED BY THE EMPEROR ZHIYOMEI ON THE OCCASION OF HIS ASCENDING MOUNT KAGU,* AND CONTEMPLATING THE SURROUNDING COUNTRY.

Countless are the mountain-chains
Tow'ring o'er Cipango's plains;
But fairest is Mount Kagu's peak,
Whose heav'nward soaring heights I seek
And gaze on all my realms beneath,—
Gaze on the land where vapours wreathe
O'er many a cot; gaze on the sea,
Where cry the seagulls merrily.
Yes! 'tis a very pleasant land,
Fill'd with joys on either hand,
Sweeter than aught beneath the sky,
Dear islands of the dragon-fly! †

---

* Near Nara.

† One of the ancient names of Japan, given to the country on account of a supposed resemblance in shape to that insect. The dragon-flies of Japan are various and very beautiful.

The Mikado's Bow.*

When the dawn is shining,
He takes it up and fondles it with pride;
When the day's declining,
He lays it by his pillow's side.
Hark to the twanging of the string!
This is the bow of our Great Lord and King!
Now to the morning chase they ride,
Now to the chase again at eventide:
Hark to the twanging of the string!
This is the bow of our Great Lord and King!
(HASHIBITO.)

Spring and Autumn.

(AN ODE COMPOSED IN OBEDIENCE TO THE COMMANDS OF THE MIKADO TEÑJI.)

When winter turns to spring,
Birds that were songless make their songs resound,
Flow'rs that were flow'rless cover all the ground;
Yet 'tis no perfect thing:—
I cannot walk, so tangled is each hill;
So thick the herbs, I cannot pluck my fill.
But in the autumn-tide
I cull the scarlet leaves and love them dear,
And let the green leaves stay, with many a tear,
All on the fair hill-side:—

* The Mikado referred to is Zhiyomei, who died in A.D. 641.

No time so sweet as that. Away! away!
Autumn's the time I fain would keep alway.
(OHOGIMI.)

Spring.

When winter turns to spring,
The dews of morn in pearly radiance lie,
The mists of eve rise circling to the sky,
And Kaminábi's thickets ring
With the sweet notes the nightingale doth sing.
(ANON.)

The Brook of Hatsuse.

Pure is Hatsúse's mountain-brook,—
So pure it mirrors all the clouds of heaven;
Yet here no fishermen for shelter look
When sailing home at even:
'Tis that there are no sandy reaches,
Nor shelving beaches,
Where the frail craft might find some shelt'ring nook.

Ah, well-a-day! we have no sandy reaches:
But heed that not;
Nor shelving beaches:
But heed that not!

Come a jostling and a hustling
O'er our billows gaily bustling:
Come, all ye boats, and anchor in this spot!
(ANON.)

Lines to a Friend.

Japan is not a land where men need pray,
For 'tis itself divine:—
Yet do I lift my voice in prayer and say:
"May ev'ry joy be thine!

And may I too, if thou those joys attain,
Live on to see thee blest!"
Such the fond prayer, that, like the restless main,
Will rise within my breast.
(HITOMARO.)

[Japan is the dwelling-place of the gods, and the whole nation claims divine ancestry. Thus prayer, with them, were doubly useless. The gods are already on earth, therefore no petitions need be lifted up to heaven. Also the heart of man,—at least of Japanese man,—is naturally perfect: therefore he has only to follow the dictates of his heart, and he will do right. These are the tenets of Sintooism,* claimed by the Japanese as their aboriginal religion, but in which any person conversant with the writings of the Chinese sages will not fail to detect the influence of their ways of thought. The believers in Sintooism, moreover, are by no means consistent; for, while deprecating the use of prayer, they have numerous and lengthy liturgies. A translation of some of these liturgies and an account of the modern attempt

* Properly *Shiñ-tau* ("the Way of the Gods").

to infuse such new vitality into Sintooism as might enable it to cope with the more potent influence of the Buddhist religion, will be found in some learned essays by Mr. Ernest Satow, printed in the "Transactions of the Asiatic Society of Japan."]

The Bridge to Heaven.*

Oh! that that ancient bridge
Hanging 'twixt heaven and earth were longer still!
Oh! that yon mountain-ridge
So boldly tow'ring tow'red more boldly still!
Then from the moon on high
I'd fetch some drops of the life-giving stream,†—
A gift that might beseem
Our Lord the King, to make him live for aye!

(Anon.)

A Very Ancient Ode.

Mountains and ocean-waves
Around me lie;
For ever the mountain-chains
Tower to the sky;

---

* The poet alludes to the so-called *ama no ukihashi*, or "floating bridge of heaven,"—the bridge by which, according to the Japanese mythology, the gods passed up and down in the days of old. The idea of such bridges seems to have been common in early times in Japan, for there are several traditions concerning them in various widely-separated provinces.

† The translator can discover no reference elsewhere to this lunar river or spring. The commentator Mabuchi says: "The poet uses this expression on account of the watery nature of the moon."

Fixed is the ocean
Immutably:—
Man is a thing of nought,
Born but to die!

(ANON.)

The Seventh Night of the Seventh Moon.

[The following poem requires some elucidation. The "Heavenly River" is the Milky Way. The Herdboy is a star in Aquila, and the Weaver is the star Vega. The fable of their being spouses or lovers who may never meet but on the seventh night of the seventh moon is extremely ancient, apparently owing its origin to some allusions to the movements of the two stars in question in the "*She King*," or "Book of Ancient Chinese Poetry," edited by Confucius. As might be expected, the legend has taken several forms. According to one version, the Weaver was a maiden who dwelt on the left bank of the River of Heaven, and was so constantly employed in making garments for the offspring of the Emperor of Heaven (God), that she had no leisure to attend to the adorning of her person. At last, however, God, taking compassion on her loneliness, gave her in marriage to a Herdsman who dwelt upon the opposite bank of the stream. Hereupon the Weaver began to grow slack in her work; and God in his anger made her recross the river, at the same time forbidding her husband to visit her more than once every year. Another story represents the pair as having been mortals who were married at the ages of fifteen and twelve, and who died at the ages of a hundred and three and ninety-nine respectively. After death, their spirits flew up to the sky, in the river watering which, the supreme divinity was unfortunately in the habit of performing his ablutions daily. No mortals, therefore, might pollute it by their touch, excepting on the seventh day of the seventh moon, when the deity, instead of bathing, went to listen to the reading of the Buddhist scriptures. Japanese literature, like that of China, teems with allusions to

the loves of the Herdboy and the Weaver; and till within the last three or four years, the seventh day of the seventh moon was one of the most popular festivals in town and country. Traces of it, as of almost everything else that was picturesque and quaint, must now be sought for in the remoter provincial districts.]

Since the hour when first begun
Heaven and earth their course to run,
Parted by the Heav'nly River
Stand the Herdboy and the Weaver:
For in each year these lovers may
Meet but for one single day.
To and fro the constant swain
Wanders in the heavenly plain,
Till sounds the hour when fore and aft
He's free to deck his tiny craft
In gallant trim, and ship the oar
To bear him to the opposing shore.
  Now the autumn season leads,
When through the swaying, sighing reeds
Rustles the chill breath of even,
And o'er the foaming stream of heaven,
Heedless of the silv'ry spray,
He'll row exulting on his way,
And, with his arms in hers entwin'd,
Tell all the loving tale he pin'd
To tell her through the livelong year.
  Yes! the seventh moon is here;
And I, though mortal, hail the night
That brings heav'n's lovers such delight.

(Anon.)

Recollections of My Children.

[To the verses are, in the original, prefixed the following lines of prose :—

"The holy Shiyaka Muni, letting drop verities from his golden mouth, says, 'I lovo mankind as I love Ragora.'* And again he preaches, 'No love exceedeth a parent's love.' Thus even so great a saint retained his love for his child. How much more, then, shall not the common run of men love their children ?"]

Ne'er a melon can I eat,
But calls to mind my children dear;
Ne'er a chestnut crisp and sweet,
But makes the lov'd ones seem more near.
Whence did they come my life to cheer?
Before mine eyes they seem to sweep,
So that I may not even sleep.

Short Stanza on the same occasion.

What use to me the gold and silver hoard ?
What use to me the gems most rich and rare?
Brighter by far,—ay! bright beyond compare,—
The joys my children to my heart afford!

(YAMAGAMI-NO-OKURA.)

---

* Properly Rāhula, Buddha's only son. Shiyaka, a corruption of Sākya, is the name commonly employed in Japan to designate the Indian prince Gautama, the founder of Buddhism, whom Europeans usually call Buddha.

Lines

COMPOSED ON THE OCCASION OF MY LORD OHOTOMO, THE INSPECTOR OF TRIBUTE, MAKING THE ASCENT OF MOUNT TSUKÚBA.

[Who this Lord Ohotomo was is not certain, there being no sufficient grounds for supposing, with the commentator Keichiyuu, that he was the same as the Prime Minister Ohotomo mentioned on page 105 as father of the poetess Sakanouhe. Mount Tsukuba, in the province of Hitachi, is well seen from Yedo, rising with its two peaks of almost exactly equal height, at a distance of some sixty miles to the north of the city, and gaining from the flatness of the country, between its base and the coast, an appearance of dignity to which its actual elevation of only three thousand feet would scarcely entitle it. The translator, on making the ascent, found a small shrine on either peak, one dedicated to the god, and the other to the goddess, of the locality.]

When my lord, who fain would look on
Great Tsukúba, double-crested,
To the highlands of Hitáchi
Bent his steps, then I, his servant,
Panting with the heats of summer,
Down my brow the sweat-drops dripping,
Breathlessly toil'd onward, upward,
Tangled roots of timber clutching.
"There, my lord! behold the prospect!"
Cried I when we scal'd the summit.
And the gracious goddess gave us
Smiling welcome, while her consort
Condescended to admit us
Into these his sacred precincts,
O'er Tsukuba double-crested,
Where the clouds do have their dwelling

And the rain for ever raineth,
Shedding his divine refulgence,
And revealing to our vision
Ev'ry landmark that in darkness
And in shapeless gloom was shrouded;—
Till for joy our belts we loosen'd,
Casting off constraint, and sporting
As at home we oft had sported.
Danker now than in the dulcet
Spring-time grew the summer grasses;
Yet to-day our bliss was boundless.

Couplet.

When the great men of old pass'd by this way,
Could e'en their pleasures vie with ours to-day?
(ANON.)

Ode to the Cuckoo.

Nightingales built the nest
Where, as a lonely guest,
First thy young head did rest,
Cuckoo so dear!
Strange to the father bird,
Strange to the mother bird
Sounded the note they heard,
Tender and clear.

Fleeing thy natal bow'rs
Bright with the silv'ry flow'rs,*
Oft in the summer hours
Hither thou fliest;
Light'st on some orange † tall,
Scatt'ring the blossoms all,
And, while around they fall,
Ceaselessly criest.

Though through the livelong day
Soundeth thy roundelay,
Never its accents may
Pall on mine ear:
Come, take a bribe of me!
Ne'er to far regions flee;
Dwell on mine orange-tree,
Cuckoo so dear!

(ANON.)

Ode

COMPOSED ON THE OCCASION OF ASCENDING MOUNT TSUKUBA, AND JOINING IN THE CHORIC DANCE.

Where many an eagle builds her nest
On Tsukuba's mountain-crest,
There the men and maids foregather,
And this the song they sing together:

---

* Literally "the blossoms of the *u* shrub (*deutzia sieboldiana*), which are white.

† Literally, the *tachibana* (*citrus mandarinus*), one of the orange tribe.

"I your mistress mean to woo!
You may take and love mine too!
For the gods that here do throne
Ne'er this ancient use disown:
So shut your eyes but for to-day,
And find no fault howe'er we play!

(Mushimaro.)

Ode

RESPECTFULLY PRESENTED TO PRINCE TACHIBANA-NO-HIRONARI ON THE OCCASION OF HIS DEPARTURE AS AMBASSADOR TO THE COURT OF CHINA, WISHING HIM A PROSPEROUS VOYAGE AND A HAPPY RETURN. (A.D. 733.)

In the great days of old,
When o'er the land the gods held sov'reign sway,
Our fathers lov'd to say
That the bright gods with tender care enfold
The fortunes of Japan,
Blessing the land with many an holy spell:
And what they lov'd to tell
We of this later age ourselves do prove;
For every living man
May feast his eyes on tokens of their love.

Countless are the hosts attendant
On the heav'n-establish'd throne
Of the Mikado, bright descendant
Of the goddess of the Sun:
But on thee his special grace
Lights to-day, for thou canst trace

From king to king thy noble birth
To the lords of all the earth;
And to thee the word is given
Sacred missives to convey
From the resplendent Son of Heaven
To the far distant limits of Cathay.

May the great immortals dwelling
On the isles that line thy road,
And the gods who in the swelling
Billows make their dread abode,
Gather round and safely guide thee,
While, that nought but good betide thee,
That Great Spirit * in whose hand
Lie the fortunes of our land,
And all the gods of heaven and earth,
Flutt'ring down on airy pinions,
From the country of thy birth
Waft thee to Cathay's unknown dominions!

And when, thine embassage concluded,
Hither again thou think'st to come,
May the same great gods that brooded
O'er thy going, bring thee home;

* What divinity should be understood by this term is a matter of debate among the native commentators. Probably it refers to Ohoanamuchi, the aboriginal monarch of the province of Idzumo, who, according to the national traditions, peacefully relinquished the sovereignty of the country to the Mikado's ancestors, the heaven-descended gods, on the condition of receiving from them divine honours. One of the most interesting questions connected with the semi-fabulous early Japanese history is that, as to whether this tradition may be interpreted so as to warrant the belief of the existence in Japan of a pre-Japanese civilisation.

May their fingers help thy vessel
Surely with the waves to wrestle,
As if across the azure line
Thy path were ruled with ink and line,—
That, round bold Chika's headland * turning,
Soon thou land on Mitsu's shore.
Oh! tarry not! for thee we're yearning;
On thee may Heav'n its richest blessings pour!
(YAMAGAMI-NO OKURA.)

Another Ode

PRESENTED TO THE PRINCE ON THE SAME OCCASION.

Till the thread of life is broken
Shall thine image fill my heart;
But the sov'reign lord* has spoken,
And, poor mortals, we must part!

Where the crane, with accents wailing,
On Naníha's billowy strand
Calls his mate when day is failing,
There thou leav'st thy native land.

With the foam-capped waves to wrestle,
In his place each oarsman sits;

---

* A cape in the province of Hizeñ, not far from the site of the modern town of Nagasaki. This is a long way from Mitsu-no-Hama, near Nara, the vessel's final destination; but the worst portion of the journey from China would be overpast, as the rest of the way lies through the Inland Sea.

† Not God or fate, but the Mikado.

Rounding Mitsu's cape, thy vessel
  On past countless islands flits.

While, the sacred emblems taking *
  To implore the heav'nly train,
I await thee: heed mine aching
  Heart, and soon come home again!
(KASA-NO-KANAMURA ASOÑ.)

Lines

COMPOSED ON THE OCCASION OF PRINCE WOSA'S HUNTING PARTY ON THE MOOR OF KARIJI.†

[Prince Wosa was son of the Emperor Teñmu, and died A.D. 715.]

When our prince, the mighty monarch,
When our prince, of high-set splendour,
To the hunt, with many a horseman,
Marches o'er Kariji's moorland,
Kneeling low, the deer adore him,
Kneeling low, the quails surround him.
  We, too, kneel like deer before him,
We, too, kneel like quails around him,
Giving true and trembling service;

---

* See the note to p. 77.

† *Kariji* is by some taken as a common noun in the sense of "hunting field;" but it is better to regard it as the name of a place, probably situated in the neighbourhood of the modern village of Shishiji in the province of Yamato.

And our eyes and hearts, uplifted,
Seem to rest on heav'n's own radiance,
Ever piercing new perfections
In our prince, the mighty monarch!

(HITOMARO.)

Ode to Fusiyama.*

There on the border, where the land of Kahi †
Doth touch the frontier of Suruga's land,
A beauteous province stretch'd on either hand,
See Fusiyama rear his head on high!

The clouds of heav'n in rev'rent wonder pause,
Nor may the birds those giddy heights assay,
Where melt thy snows amid thy fires away,
Or thy fierce fires lie quench'd beneath thy snows.

What name might fitly tell, what accents sing,
Thine awful, godlike grandeur? 'Tis thy breast
That holdeth Narusáha's flood at rest,
Thy side whence Fuzhikáha's waters spring.

---

* *Fusiyama* has been considered as a naturalised English word, like Vienna, Brussels, &c., and the native spelling of *Fuzhiyama* (more correctly *Fuzhinone* or *Fuzhisañ*) has therefore not been adopted in the text. *Fuzhikaha* is the name of a river, and Narusaha that of a lake now dried up. The lovely waterfalls of *Shiraito-no-Taki*, which form by far the most charming feature of the landscape surrounding the great volcano (not yet extinct in the poet's time), have been strangely passed over in silence by him as by the other poets his contemporaries. It is a common Japanese saying that no good verses have been written on Fusiyama.

† Pronounced as one syllable, as if written *Kye*. Kahi and Suruga are the names of provinces.

Great Fusiyama, tow'ring to the sky!
A treasure art thou giv'n to mortal man,
A god-protector watching o'er Japan:—
On thee for ever let me feast mine eye!

(ANON.)

Verses

COMPOSED ON THE OCCASION OF AN IMPERIAL PROGRESS TO THE SUMMER PALACE OF YOSHINO IN A.D. 725.

[Yóshino is justly famous for its beauty,—a beauty so marvellous when, in the spring-time, every mountain and every valley is ablaze with flowering trees, that, borrowing the proverb relating to Naples, it might well be said, "See Yóshino and die!" It is situated in the province of Yamato, and has witnessed some of the most stirring events of Japanese history. During the fourteenth century, when what the author of "The Mikado's Empire" has aptly termed the "Wars of the Chrysanthemums" * split up the court and country into two hostile camps, Yóshino was the residence of the southern or legitimate sovereigns, and the lovely country surrounding it was the scene of perpetual bloody combats and hairbreadth escapes. Not far from Yóshino lie the maple-trees of Tatsuta, the heights of Mount Kagu, Nara the ancient capital, all celebrated in Japanese song and story, while the palaces of Kiyauto and the blue waters of the lute-shaped lake of Afumi are not far to seek.]

Beauteous is the woody mountain
  Of imperial Yóshino;
Fair and limpid is the fountain
  Dashing to the vale below;

---

* The chrysanthemum flower is the Mikado's crest.

High beside whose upper reaches
  Warbles many a tiny bird,
While upon its lower beaches
  Frogs' loud am'rous notes are heard.*

Far and near, in stately leisure,
  Pass the courtiers o'er the lea;
Ev'ry glance shows some new pleasure,
  And I pray thus tremblingly:

"Glorious deities that for ever
  O'er the heav'n and earth do reign!
Grant that these our joys may never
  From fair Yóshino be ta'en!"

(KASA-NO-KANAMURA ASOÑ.)

[In the first moon of the fourth year of the period Zhiñki (A.D. 727), the nobles and courtiers had assembled in the fields of Kasuga,† and were diverting themselves with a game of polo, when the sky was suddenly overcast, and the rain poured down amid thunder and lightning, while the palace was left without guards or attendants. Thereupon the Mikado issued an edict confining the offenders to the guard-house, under strict prohibition of leaving its gates. The following ode was composed under the feeling of disappointment and vexation thus engendered.]

Spring his gentle beams is flinging
  O'er Kasúga's ivy-tangled lea;

* The musical (?) voice of the frog is much admired by the Japanese, and is frequently alluded to in their poetry. They also, like the ancient Greeks, have a partiality for the cry of certain species of *cicadæ*.

† Close to Nara.

To the hills the mists are clinging,
Takamáto's heights are ringing
With the nightingale's first melody.

All the court * for this entrancing
Hour had yearn'd—oh! might it never end!—
Then upon our chargers prancing,
Gaily side by side advancing,
Through the fields our course we long'd to bend.

Ah! could we have been foreknowing
This accurs'd, unutterable thing,
Then by Saho's waters flowing,
Where the ferns and rushes growing
Line the strand 'mid birds' sweet carolling,

O'er our heads their branches twining,
In the stream we might have lav'd us free: †
Now the monarch's law, confining,
Bids us mourn away the shining
Hours of spring in dark captivity.

(ANON.)

---

* The lines in the original answering to the commencement of this stanza are so corrupt as to be well-nigh unintelligible. Motowori's interpretation has been followed in the translation.

† One of the ceremonies of purification consisted in waving ferns and rushes over the person and then flinging them into the water. At a later period, for these plants were substituted the so-called *nusa* or *gohei*, strips of linen, and afterwards of paper. Religious ablutions are constantly referred to in the earliest poetry and history of the Japanese.

Ode

WHICH, AT A PARTING FEAST, THE EMPEROR SHIYAUMU * CONDESCENDED TO COMPOSE FOR THREE NOBLES ABOUT TO START ON THEIR SEVERAL CIRCUITS THROUGH THE PROVINCES. (A.D. 732.)

If, like loyal men, ye up and carry
To far realms your sov'reign lord's behest,
I within these halls of bliss may tarry,
I my hands may fold upon my breast.

O'er your heads my sacred hands, extended,
Shall caress, shall bless each faithful soul:
When ye come again, your labours ended,
I, the king, will fill again this bowl.

Lament on Nara, the Deserted Capital.†

Yamato's land, that still with pow'r imperial
Our monarchs rule in undivided sway,

* Reigned A.D. 724–756. As stated in the Introduction, it is to the reign of this prince that the "Collection of Ten Thousand Leaves" should almost certainly be referred. A note appended to the ode in the original mentions that, according to some authorities, it was composed, not by Shiyaumu himself, but by his mother, the Empress Dowager Geñshiyau, who had governed from 715 to 723, and then abdicated in favour of her son. In this case, the word "king" in the translation would have to be altered to "queen." The Japanese language, which ignores our distinction of genders, cannot here lend to criticism the assistance of grammar.

† The seat of government was definitively moved from Nara in A.D. 784, and continued to be at Kiyauto from that time until 1868.

Since first the gods came down from realms ethereal*
Hath never ceas'd those monarchs to obey.

Wherefore methought that while, in grand succession,
Prince after prince should rule earth's wide domain,
Throughout the myriad ages' long procession
From Nara's palace would they choose to reign.†

Sweet Nara! still in Mount Mikasa's bowers,
When circling mists proclaimed the pow'r of spring,
Dark'ning the forest bloomed the cherry-flowers,
Nor ever ceas'd the birds their carolling.

Still, when mid-autumn's frost-touch'd dews were falling,
High on Ikoma's ‡ often-burning crest
The lusty stag, for his dear consort calling,
O'er trampled lespedeza thickets press'd.§

Never thy hills might tire my gaze, and never
Far from thy dwellings might I wish to roam;

---

* The first sovereign of the dynasty of the gods on earth, according to the Japanese mythology, was His Grandeur Minigi, to whom the more ancient aboriginal ruler Ohoanamuchi resigned his throne and domain (see note to p. 97).

† Nara being in the province of Yamato.

‡ A mountain in the province of Kahachi, on whose summit, in ancient times, signal fires used to be lighted. Though discontinued nearly a century before the probable date of this poem, the ancient custom had bequeathed its name to one of the peaks, which was called Tobu-hi-ga-Woka, or the "Eminence of the Flying Fires."

§ In the later poetry the lespedeza flower is itself perpetually termed the stag's mate, doubtless on account of its blossoming at the time of year when these animals pair off.

Thy streets, stretch'd out across the plain for ever,
Each house some loyal and sturdy warrior's home.

And so I trusted that, till old and hoary,
The heav'ns and earth should on each other fall,
Nara might sparkle with perennial glory,
And Nara's palace hold the Lord of all.

But Nara, too, must yield, as yield all mortals,
To the great King's inscrutable commands:
Her beauty fades; the court deserts her portals,
Like birds of passage seeking other lands.

Here in these streets, where high-born throngs advancing,
And neighing steeds erst made the heav'ns resound,
No step is heard, no chargers more are prancing,
And desolation covers all the ground.

(SAKIMARO.)

A Stag's Lament.

[The following lines, and others which set forth in a similar strain the "Lamentations of a Crab," appear to have been composed with the intention of enforcing the Buddhist doctrine of the sinfulness of slaying any living creature. The first ten lines in the original offer a good example of the poetical ornament described in the Introduction under the name of a "preface," forming, as they do, a mere preparation for the "pillow-word" which ushers in the name of Mount Heguri.]

Oft in June, or earlier May-tide,
On Heguri's heights foregather
From afar the med'cine hunters,*
Where, amidst the mountain gorges,
By twin-soaring yew-trees shelter'd,
As with many a stalwart comrade,
Arm'd with bows and arm'd with arrows,
For the passing deer I waited,
Came a stag, and stood before me,
And thus 'gan his lamentation:—
"Sudden death is now my sentence;
I must serve the mighty monarch,
And mine horns shall grace his sunshade,
And mine ears shall be his inkhorn,
And mine eyes shall be his mirror,
And mine hoofs shall be his bow-notch,
And mine hairs shall grace his pencil,
And mine hide shall line his casket,
And my flesh shall be his mincemeat,
And my liver, too, his mincemeat,
And my cud shall be his seas'ning.
Men shall praise me, men shall praise me,
Saying, 'Lo! on one poor agèd
Stag these sev'nfold blossoms flower,
Eightfold blossoms flower sweetly!'" †

(Anon.)

* The flesh of the stag was supposed to possess medicinal properties.

† What in English are called "double-flowers" are termed by the Japanese "eightfold flowers." The "sevenfold" is in the original put merely to fill up the verse, and has no special meaning.

Lines

COMPOSED WHEN THE POET COULD NOT CONTAIN HIMSELF FOR JOY AT HAVING BEHELD IN A DREAM A FAVOURITE HAWK THAT HE HAD LOST.*

Farthest of all the lands that own
The sov'reign monarch's might,
There lies a province wild and lone,
"Koshi the Snowy" hight.

So barren are its moors, that nought
But tangled grasses grow;
So high its hills, that like mere rills
The distant rivers show.

There, when on panting summer night
The grayling dart around,
With cormorants and lanterns bright
Into their wherries bound

The fishermen, a merry crowd,
From off the shingly beach,
And row against the dashing flood
Though ev'ry crystal reach.

And when the hoar-frost 'gins to fall,
And Koshi's autumn moors
Are full of birds, my hawkers all
Assemble out of doors.

* The poet, at the time of composing this piece, was governor of the province of Koshi in the north-west of the empire.

But none of their so vaunted stock
  With "Blackie" mote compare :—
"Big Blackie" was a roof-tailed hawk,
  And a silver bell she bare.

At morn five hundred birds we'd start,
  And more at fall of day:
Swift in her flight, swift to alight,
  She never miss'd her prey.

But while I gaz'd with smiling pride
  Upon my "Blackie" dear,
Sure that in all the world beside
  Ne'er would arise her peer,

That ugly, vile, and craz'd old man,*
  All on a rainy day,
Without a word, takes the dear bird
  Out hunting far away;

And, coming back, and coughing low,
  Tells me the bitter tale,
How, soaring from the moor below,
  Heav'nward the hawk did sail,

On past Mishíma's grassy plain
  And Futagámi's height,
Till, lost amid the clouds and rain,
  She vanish'd from the sight.

---

* My lord's hawker.

To tempt her home was past my pow'r :
   Helpless and dumb I stood,
While flames my bosom did devour,
   And sadly I did brood.

And yet, if haply some fond spell
   Might lure her back to me,
Watchers I set, and many a net
   All over hill and lea;

And with the holy symbols white,
   And glitt'ring mirror's sphere,*
Call'd on the gods of awful might
   My sad complaint to hear.

So, as I waited at the shrine,
   And sleep stole o'er mine eyes,
A fairy maid stood forth and said :—
   " The hawk thy soul doth prize,

" Thy glorious 'Blackie,' is not lost;
   But o'er Matsúda's beach,
And where the fisher-boats are toss'd
   On Himi's breezy reach,

" O'er Furu's strand and Tako's isle,
   Where myriad seagulls play,
She's been a hunting all the while :
   I saw her yesterday.

---

* For the use of the mirror and of linen or paper symbols in making supplication to the gods see the notes to pp. 77 and 103.

"Two days at least must come and go
  Before she homeward flies;
Sev'n days at most,—it must be so,—
  Will show her to thine eyes.

"So let thy tears no longer stream,
  No more for 'Blackie' sigh!"
So spake the maiden in my dream,
  Then vanish'd to the sky.

(YAKAMOCHI.)

[In the year 749 there had been no rain since the sixth day of the intercalary fifth moon,* and the peasants' fields and gardens seemed on the point of drying up. On the first day of the sixth moon there suddenly appeared a rain-cloud, which gave occasion to the following verses.]

From ev'ry quarter of the vast domains,—
Earth's whole expanse,—o'er which the sov'reign
  reigns,
Far as the clank of horses' hoofs resounds,
Far as the junks seek ocean's utmost bounds,
Ten thousand off'rings, as in days of yore,
Still to this day their varied treasures pour
Into th' imperial coffers:—but of all
The bearded rice is chief and principal.
But now, alas! the fields are till'd in vain;

---

* According to the old Japanese calendar, which was modelled on that of China, an intercalary month had to be inserted three times in every eight years to make up for the reckoning of the year as containing only 360 days.

Day follows day, and still no show'r of rain;
Morn after morn each thirsty blade droops down,
And ev'ry garden tint is chang'd to brown;
While I, heart-stricken, on the prospect gaze,
And, as the infant that his hands doth raise
To clutch his mother's breast, so to the heav'n
I lift mine eyes to pray that rain be giv'n.
Oh! may the cloud whose fleecy form is seen
To rest yon distant mountain-peaks between,
Wafted across to where the ocean-god
Makes in the foaming waves his dread abode,
Meet with the vapours of the wat'ry plain,
Then here returning, fall as grateful rain!
(YAKAMOCHI.)

Lament on the Mutability of all Earthly Things.

Since the far natal hour of earth and heaven,
Men never cease to cry
That ne'er to aught in this our world 'twas given
To last eternally.

If upward gazing on the moon of light
That hangs in heav'n's high plain,
I see her wax, 'twill not be many a night
Before that moon shall wane.

And if in spring each twig puts forth his flow'r
On all the hills around,
Dew-chill'd and storm-swept in dull autumn's hour
The leaves fall to the ground,

Such, too, is man: soon pales the ruddy cheek,
The raven locks soon fade;
And the fresh smile of morn 'twere vain to seek
Amid the evening shade.

And I that gaze upon the mortal scene,
My tears flow down for ever,
Where all is viewless as the wind unseen,
And fleeting as the river.

(YAKAMOCHI.)

The Cuckoo.

(MAY, A.D. 750.)

Near to the valley stands my humble cot,
The village nestles 'neath the cooling shade
Of lofty timber; but the silent glade
Not yet re-echoes with the cuckoo's note.

The morning hour e'er finds me, sweetest bird!
Before my gate; and, when the day doth pale,
I cast a wistful glance adown the vale;—
But e'en one note, alas! not yet is heard.

(HIRONAHA.)

Lines

SENT BY A MOTHER TO HER DAUGHTER. (JULY, A.D. 750.)

[The mother was Sakanouhe, and lived at the court of Nara. Her daughter, who was married to the poet Yakamochi, had accompanied her husband to his governorship of the distant province of Koshi.*]

Thou wast my child, and to my heart more dear
Than to the sov'reign monarch of the deep
All the rich jewels that in casket rare
Beneath the billows he is said to keep.
But it was just that thy bold spouse should bear
Thee in his train t'ward Koshi's deserts wild.
Thou bad'st adieu; and since that hour, sweet child,
In ceaseless visions of remembrance clear
There seems to float the face for which I yearn,
The brows oblique as ocean's crested wave.
But I am old, and scarce love's pow'r to save
May stretch my life to welcome thy return.

(SAKANOUHE.)

* The native commentators do not notice the discrepancy between the statement of this poem that Yakamochi *had taken his wife with him* to his far northern governorship, and those of his own verses written from the north to the *wife whom he had left at Nara*, and lamenting his solitary state (see the songs on pp. 64 and 66, besides many others in the "*Mañyefushifu*"). The simplest explanation probably is that the poet had two wives (though Sakanouhe's daughter was doubtless the legitimate one), and that, in writing of his solitariness to his Nara wife, he made use of a poetical license as common among the ancient Japanese as the relations between the sexes were loose.

Short Stanzas

FROM THE

"KOKIÑSHIFU;"

OR,

"COLLECTION OF ODES, ANCIENT AND MODERN."

SHORT STANZAS.

I.

(*Spring*, i. 4.*)

Spring, spring, has come, while yet the landscape bears
Its fleecy burden of unmelted snow!
Now may the zephyr gently 'gin to blow,
To melt the nightingale's sweet frozen tears.

(*Anon.*)

2.

(*Spring*, i. 6.)

Amid the branches of the silv'ry bowers
The nightingale doth sing: perchance he knows
That spring hath come, and takes the later snows
For the white petals of the plum's sweet flowers.†

(SOSEI.)

---

* As noted in the Introduction, the "*Kokiñshifu*" stanzas are, in the original, arranged in several categories,—Spring, Summer, Love, &c., many of which are themselves subdivided. Thus *Spring*, i. 4, signifies the fourth ode in the first subdivision of Spring, and so on of the rest.

† The plum-tree, cherry-tree, &c., are in Japan cultivated not for their fruit, but for their blossoms. Together with the wisteria, the lotus, the iris, the lespedeza, and a few others, these take the place which is occupied in the West by the rose, the lily, the violet, &c. Though flowers are perpetually referred to and immensely admired, there has never been any symbolism connected with them.

3.

(*Spring*, i. 23.)

Too lightly woven must the garments be,—
Garments of mist,—that clothe the coming spring:
In wild disorder see them fluttering
Soon as the zephyr breathes adown the lea.

(YUKIHIRA.)

4.

(*Spring*, i. 31.)

Heedless that now the mists of spring do rise,
Why fly the wild geese northward?—Can it be
Their native home is fairer to their eyes,
Though no sweet flowers blossom on its lea?

(ISE.)

5.

(*Spring*, i. 55.)

If earth but ceas'd to offer to my sight
The beauteous cherry-trees when blossoming,
Ah! then indeed, with peaceful, pure delight,
My heart might revel in the joys of spring!*

(NARIHIRA.)

6.

(*Spring*, ii. 8.)

Tell me, doth any know the dark recess
Where dwell the winds that scatter the spring flow'rs?

---

* *i.e.*, "The cherry-blossoms are ineffably lovely; but my joy in gazing at them is marred by the knowledge that they must so soon pass away."

Hide it not from me! By the heav'nly pow'rs,
I'll search them out to upbraid their wickedness!
(SOSEI.)

7.

(*Spring*, ii. 20.)

No man so callous but he heaves a sigh
When o'er his head the wither'd cherry-flowers
Come flutt'ring down.—Who knows? the spring's soft show'rs
May be but tears shed by the sorrowing sky.
(KURONUSHI.)

8.

(*Spring*, ii. 41.)

Whom would your cries, with artful calumny,
Accuse of scatt'ring the pale cherry-flow'rs?
'Tis your own pinions flitting through these bow'rs
That raise the gust which makes them fall and die!
(SOSEI.)

9.

(*Summer*, 1.)

In blossoms the wisteria-tree to-day
Breaks forth, that sweep the wavelets of my lake:
When will the mountain-cuckoo come and make
The garden vocal with his first sweet lay? *
(*Attributed to* HITOMARO.)

---

* The wisteria among flowers, and among birds the cuckoo, are the poetical representatives of early summer, as are the plum-blossom and the nightingale of early spring.

10.

(*Summer*, 31.)

Oh, lotus-leaf! I dreamt that the wide earth
Held nought more pure than thee,—held nought more true:
Why, then, when on thee rolls a drop of dew,
Pretend that 'tis a gem of priceless worth? *

(HEÑZEU.)

11.

(*Autumn*, i. 4.)

Can I be dreaming? 'Twas but yesterday
We planted out each tender shoot again; †
And now the autumn breeze sighs o'er the plain,
Where fields of yellow rice confess its sway.

(*Anon.*)

12.

(*Autumn*, i. 25.)

A thousand thoughts of tender vague regret
Crowd on my soul, what time I stand and gaze
On the soft-shining autumn moon;—and yet
Not to me only speaks her silv'ry haze.

(CHISATO.)

---

* The lotus is the Buddhist emblem of purity, and the lotus growing out of the mud is a frequent metaphor for the heart that remains unsullied by contact with the world.

† The transplanting of the rice occupies the whole rural population during the month of June, when men and women may all be seen working in the fields knee-deep in water. The crops are gathered in October.

13.

(*Autumn*, i. 44.)

What bark impell'd by autumn's fresh'ning gale
Comes speeding t'ward me?—'Tis the wild geese driv'n
Across the fathomless expanse of Heav'n,
And lifting up their voices for a sail!

(*Anon.*)

14.

(*Autumn*, i. 58.)

The silv'ry dewdrops that in autumn light
Upon the moors must surely jewels be;
For there they hang all over hill and lea,
Strung on the threads the spiders weave so tight.

(ASAYASU.)

15.

(*Autumn*, ii. 2.)

The trees and herbage, as the year doth wane,
For gold and russet leave their former hue,—
All but the wave-toss'd flow'rets of the main,
That never yet chill autumn's empire knew.

(YASUHIDE.

16.

(*Autumn*, ii. 9.)

The dews are all of one pale silv'ry white:
Then tell me, if thou canst, oh! tell me why

These silv'ry dews so marvellously dye
The autumn leaves a myriad colours bright?
(TOSHIYUKI.)

17.

(*Autumn*, ii. 44.)

The warp is hoar-frost and the woof is dew,—
Too frail, alas! the warp and woof to be:
For scarce the woods their damask robes endue,
When, torn and soil'd, they flutter o'er the lea.
(SEKIWO.)

18.

(*Autumn*, ii. 47.)

E'en when on earth the thund'ring gods held sway
Was such a sight beheld?—Calm Tatsta's * flood,
Stain'd, as by Chinese art, with hues of blood,
Rolls o'er Yamáto's peaceful fields away.
(NARIHIRA.)

19.

(*Winter*, 10.)

When falls the snow, lo! ev'ry herb and tree,
That in seclusion through the wintry hours
Long time had been held fast, breaks forth in flow'rs
That ne'er in spring were known upon the lea.
(TSURAYUKI.)

* Properly written Tatsuta. The allusion here is to the crimson and scarlet of the autumn maple-trees, which may well form a constantly recurring theme for the raptures of the Japanese poets, who in the fall of every year see around them a halo of glory such as our dull European forests do not even distantly approach.

20.

(*Winter*, 17.)

When from the skies, that wintry gloom enshrouds,
The blossoms fall and flutter round my head,
Methinks the spring e'en now his light must shed
O'er heavenly lands that lie beyond the clouds.
(FUKAYABU.)

21.

(*Congratulations*, 1.)

A thousand years of happy life be thine!
Live on, my lord, till what are pebbles now,
By age united, to great rocks shall grow,
Whose venerable sides the moss doth line!
(*Anon.*)

22.

(*Congratulations*, 9.)

[Ode composed on beholding a screen presented to the Empress by Prince Sadayasu * at the festival held in honour of her fiftieth birthday, whereon was painted a man seated beneath the falling cherry-blossoms and watching them flutter down.]

Of all the days and months that hurry by
Nor leave a trace, how long the weary tale!

* The Empress intended is the one famous in Japanese literature under the designation of Nideu-no-Kisaki, consort of the Mikado Seiwa and mother of Prince Sadayasu. It was in A.D. 891 that the festival was held.

And yet how few the springs when in the vale
On the dear flow'rets I may feast mine eye! *
(OKIKAZE.)

23.

(*Congratulations*, 11.)

If ever mortal in the days of yore
By Heav'n a thousand years of life was lent,
I wot not; but if never seen before,
Be thou the man to make the precedent! †
(SOSEI.)

24.

(*Parting*, 39.)

Mine oft-reiterated pray'rs in vain
The parting guest would stay: Oh, cherry-flow'rs!
Pour down your petals, that from out these bow'rs
He ne'er may find the homeward path again!
(*Anon.*)

25.

(*Travelling*, 4.)

With roseate hues that pierce th' autumnal haze
The spreading dawn lights up Akashi's shore;

---

* In rendering this stanza the translator has followed, not the original "*Kokiñshifu*" text, but the better known reading of the "*Rauyeishifu*" ("Collection of Bright Songs"), a compilation made early in the eleventh century as a wedding-present for his son-in-law Michinori (afterwards regent of the empire) by the Minister Kiñtau.

† For this very prosaic expression the Japanese original is responsible.

But the fair ship, alas! is seen no more:—
An island veils it from my loving gaze.
(*Attributed to* HITOMARO,)

But more probably by some court lady who thus expresses her grief at the sight of the departure of the vessel bearing her love from her side. Akashi is a lovely spot on the shores of the Inland Sea.

26.

(*Travelling*, 6.)

[The high-born poet Narihira, who had been banished from the court on account of an intrigue with the Empress; was either compelled, or himself chose,—we know not which,—to hide his disgrace in a temporary absence from the capital, and made to what were then the wild and almost undiscovered districts of Eastern Japan, a journey whose every step has been rendered classic in the national literature through the pages of the "*Ise Mono-gatari*," an historical romance which details in the most perfect literary style Narihira's amorous and other adventures, and strings together on a thread of narrative the various odes that he composed.* "He had now," says the original, "reached the banks of the river Sumida, which floweth between the lands of Musashi and Shimofusa,† and had dismounted and sat him down awhile with his heart full of loving remembrances of Miyako, gazing steadfastly before him, and thinking of the immeasurable distance that he had travelled. Nor was there any in the whole company whose thoughts went not back to Miyako, as the ferryman bade them hasten on board for that the daylight had waned; and so they stepped into the boat. And as thus they grieved, they saw a white fowl sporting on the bank of the river,—white, with

* This is not the place to discuss, but the translator may state that he totally rejects the theory of one eminent native critic, who holds that the Narihira of literature and the Narihira of history are not the same individual. There is no warrant for such an opinion.

† On the spot where, seven and a half centuries later, rose the great city of Yedo.

red legs and a red bill; and it was a fowl never beheld in Miyako, so none of all the company did know it. So when they inquired of the ferryman its name, and Narihira heard him make answer, 'This is the Miyako-bird,' he composed this verse :]

Miyako-bird! if not in vain men give
Thy pleasing name, my question deign to hear:—
And has she pass'd away, my darling dear,
Or doth she still for Narihira live?

(NARIHIRA.)

27.

(*Acrostics*, 8.*)

Since that I talk'd with thee, my brooding heart
Is sadder far than when I was less blest:—
The prescient thought will never let me rest
Of the swift-coming hour when we must part.

(FUKAYABU.)

28.

(*Love*, i. 44.)

The barest ledge of rock, if but a seed
Alight upon it, lets the pine-tree grow:—
If, then, thy love for me be love indeed,
We'll come together, dear; it must be so!

(*Anon.*)

---

* In the English version of this stanza the general sense alone has been preserved. The play in the original is on *Kara-momo-no-hana*, the name of a flower, which is embedded in the text after the fashion of the popular game of "Buried Cities," thus:—

Afu KARA MO
MONO HA NAHO *koso*
Kanashikere,
Wakareñ koto wo
Kanete omoheba.

29.

(*Love*, i. 54.)

There is on earth a thing more bootless still
Than to write figures on a running stream:
And that thing is (believe me if you will)
To dream of one who ne'er of you doth dream.

(*Anon.*)

30.

(*Love*, i. 66.*)

Now hid from sight are great Mount Fusi's fires.
Mount Fusi, said I ?—'Tis myself I mean;
For the word *Fusi* signifies, I ween,
Few see the constant flame of my desires.

(*Anon.*)

31.

(*Love*, ii. 2.)

Since that first night when, bath'd in hopeless tears,
I sank asleep, and he I love did seem
To visit me, I welcome ev'ry dream,
Sure that they come as heav'n-sent messengers.

(KOMACHI.)

32.

(*Love*, ii. 9.)

Methinks my tenderness the grass must be,
Clothing some mountain desolate and lone;

* This stanza is, by the necessity of the case, a mere free imitation of the punning original.

For though it daily grows luxuriantly,
To ev'ry mortal eye 'tis still unknown.

(YOSHIKI.)

33.

(*Love*, ii. 23.)

Upon the causeway through the land of dreams
Surely the dews must plentifully light;
For when I've wander'd up and down all night,
My sleeve's so wet that nought will dry its streams.

(TSURAYUKI.)

34.

(*Love*, ii. 43.)

Fast fall the silv'ry dews, albeit not yet
'Tis autumn weather; for each drop's a tear,
Shed till the pillow of my hand is wet,
As I wake from dreaming of my dear.

(*Anon.*)

35.

(*Love*, v. 56.)

I ask'd my soul where springs th' ill-omened seed
That bears the herb of dull forgetfulness; *
And answer straightway came: Th' accursed weed
Grows in that heart which knows no tenderness.

(SOSEI.)

* The "Herb of Forgetfulness" (*wasure-gusa*) answers in the poetical diction of the Japanese to the classical waters of Lethe.

36.

(*Elegies*, 10.*)

So frail our life, perchance to-morrow's sun
May never rise for me. Ah! well-a-day!
Till comes the twilight of the sad to-day,
I'll mourn for thee, O thou beloved one!

(TSURAYUKI.)

37.

(*Elegies*, 23.)

The perfume is the same, the same the hue
As that which erst my senses did delight:
But he who planted the fair avenue
Is here no more, alas! to please my sight!

(TSURAYUKI.)

38.

(*Elegies*, 31.)

One thing, alas! more fleeting have I seen
Than wither'd leaves driv'n by the autumn gust:
Yea, evanescent as the whirling dust
Is man's brief passage o'er this mortal scene!

(CHISATO.)

---

* It is the young poet Ki-no-Tomonori who is mourned in this stanza. He was nephew to Tsurayuki, and, after holding several high posts at court, had been appointed to assist his uncle in the compilation of the "Odes Ancient and Modern." He died in A.D. 905, a few months before the completion of the work.

39.

(*Miscellaneous*, i. 1.)

Softly the dews upon my forehead light:
From off the oars, perchance, as feather'd spray,
They drop, while some fair skiff bends on her way
Across the Heav'nly Stream * on starlit night.
(*Anon.*)

40.

(*Miscellaneous*, i. 24.)

What though the waters of that antique rill
That flows along the heath no more are cold;
Those who remember what it was of old
Go forth to draw them in their buckets still.
(*Anon.*)

41.

(*Miscellaneous*, i. 33.†)

Old Age is not a friend I wish to meet;
And if some day to see me he should come,
I'd lock the door as he walk'd up the street,
And cry, "Most honour'd sir! I'm not at home!"
(*Anon.*)

---

* The Milky Way.

† This stanza is remarkable for being (so far as the present writer is aware) the only instance in Japanese literature of that direct impersonation of an abstract idea which is so very strongly marked a characteristic of Western thoughts and modes of expression.

42.

(*Miscellaneous*, i. 41.*)

Yes, I am old; but yet with doleful stour
I will not choose to rail 'gainst Fate's decree.
An' I had not grown old, then ne'er for me
Had dawn'd the day that brings this golden hour.

(TOSHIYUKI.)

43.

(*Miscellaneous*, i. 61.†)

The roaring torrent scatters far and near
Its silv'ry drops :—Oh! let me pick them up!
For when of grief I drain some day the cup,
Each will do service as a bitter tear.

(YUKIHIRA.)

44.

(*Miscellaneous*, i. 64.)

[Composed on beholding the cascade of Otoha on Mount Hiye.]

Long years, methinks, of sorrow and of care
Must have pass'd over the old fountain-head
Of the cascade; for like a silv'ry thread
It rolls adown, nor shows one jet black hair.

(TADAMINE.)

45.

(*Miscellaneous*, ii. 24.)

If e'en that grot where thou didst seek release
From worldly strife in lonesome mountain glen

---

* Composed on the occasion of a feast at the palace.

† One of a number of stanzas composed by a party of courtiers who visited the cascade of Nunobiki, near the site of the modern treaty-port of Kaube.

Should find thee sometimes sorrowful, ah! then
Where mayst thou farther flee to search for peace?
(MITSUNE.)

46.

(*Conceits*, 11.)

[Stanza composed and sent to the owner of the neighbouring house on the last day of winter, when the wind had blown some snow across from it into the poet's dwelling.]

So close thy friendly roof, so near the spring,
That though not yet dull winter hath gone hence,
The wind that bloweth o'er our parting fence
From thee to me the first gay flow'rs doth bring.
(FUKAYABU.)

47.

(*Conceits*, 21.)

If to this frame of mine in spring's first hour,
When o'er the moor the lightsome mists do curl,
Might but be lent the shape of some fair flower,
Haply thou'dst deign to pluck me, cruel girl!
(OKIKAZE.)

48.

(*Conceits*, 29.)

"Love me, sweet girl! thy love is all I ask!"
"Love thee?" she laughing cries; "I love thee not!"
"Why, then I'll cease to love thee on the spot,
Since loving thee is such a thankless task!"
(*Anon.*)

49.

(*Conceits,* 31.)

A youth once lov'd me, and his love I spurn'd.
But see the vengeance of the pow'rs above
On cold indiff'rence: now 'tis I that love,
And my fond love, alas! is not return'd.

(*Anon.*)

50.

(*Conceits,* 48.)

Beneath love's heavy weight my falt'ring soul
Plods, like the packman, o'er life's dusty road.
Oh! that some friendly hand would find a pole
To ease my shoulders of their grievous load!

(*Anon.*)

Selections

FROM THE

NOU-NO-UTAHI;"

OR,

"*LYRIC DRAMAS.*"

---

1. THE ROBE OF FEATHERS.
2. THE DEATH STONE.
3. LIFE IS A DREAM.
4. NAKAMITSU.

The Robe of Feathers.

DRAMATIS PERSONÆ.

A FAIRY. A FISHERMAN. THE CHORUS.

SCENE.—The shore of Miho,* in the province of Suruga, near the base of Fusiyama.

[*The piece opens with a long recitative in which the Fisherman and the Chorus describe the beauties of Miho's pine-clad shore at dawn in spring. The passage is a beautiful one; but, after several efforts at reproducing it in an English form, the translator has had to abandon the task as impossible. At the conclusion of this recitative the Fisherman steps on shore, and the action of the piece then commences as follows:* †—]

Fisherman. As I land on Miho's pine-clad shore and gaze around me, flowers come fluttering down

---

* Pronounced like the Italian word *mio.*

† The end of the poetical opening of the piece is perhaps fairly rendered by the following lines:—

But hark! methought I saw the storm-clouds flying
  And heard the tempest rave:
Come, fishermen! come homeward plying!—
  But no! no tempest frets the wave:
'Tis spring! 'tis spring! 'twas but the morning breeze,
  That vocal grew th' eternal pines among;
No murmur rises from th' unruffled seas,
  No storm disturbs the thronging boatmen's song!

from the ethereal space, strains of music are re-echoing, and a more than earthly fragrance fills the air. Surely there is something strange in this. Yes! from one of the branches of yonder pine-tree hangs a beauteous robe, which, when I draw nigh and closely scan it, reveals itself more fair and fragrant than any common mortal garb. Let me take it back to show to the old folks in the village, that it may be handed down in our house as an heirloom for all generations.

Fairy. Ah! mine is that apparel! Wherefore wouldst thou carry it away?

Fisherman. 'Twas found by me, forsooth, and I shall take it home with me.

Fairy. But 'tis a fairy's robe of feathers, a thing that may not lightly be bestowed on any mortal being. Prithee leave it on the branch from which it hung.

Fisherman. What, then, art thou thyself a fairy, that thou claimest possession of this feathery raiment? As a marvel for all ages will I keep it, and garner it up among the treasures of Japan. No, no! I cannot think of restoring it to thee.

Fairy. Alas! without my robe of feathers never more can I go soaring through the realms of air, never more can I return to my celestial home. I beg thee, *I beseech thee,* therefore, to give it back to me.

Fisherman. Nay, fairy, nay, the more I hear thee plead
The more my soul determines on the deed;
My cruel breast but grows more heartless yet;
Thou mayst not have thy feathers: 'tis too late.

Fairy. Speak not, dear fisherman! speak not that word!
Ah! know'st thou not that, like the hapless bird

Whose wings are broke, I seek, but seek in vain,
Reft of my wings, to soar to heav'n's blue plain?

Fisherman. Chain'd to dull earth a fairy well may pine.

Fairy. Whichever way I turn, despair is mine:

Fisherman. For ne'er the fisher will her wings restore,

Fairy. And the frail fay sinks helpless evermore.

Chorus. Alas! poor maiden, in thy quiv'ring eyne
Cluster the dews; the flow'rets thou didst twine
Amidst thy tresses languish and decay,
And the five woes * declare thy fatal day!

Fairy. Vainly my glance doth seek the heav'nly plain,
Where rising vapours all the air enshroud,
And veil the well-known paths from cloud to cloud.

Chorus. Clouds! wand'ring clouds! she yearns, and yearns in vain,
Soaring like you, to tread the heav'ns again;

---

* *Viz.*, the withering of the crown of flowers, the pollution by dust of the heavenly raiment, a deadly sweat, a feeling of dizzy blindness, and the loss of all joy.

Vainly she sighs to hear, as erst she heard,
The melting strains of Paradise' sweet bird: *
That blessèd voice grows faint. The heav'n in vain
Rings with the song of the returning crane;
In vain she lists, where ocean softly laves,
To the free seagull twitt'ring o'er the waves;
Vainly she harks where zephyr sweeps the plain:
These all may fly, but she'll ne'er fly again!

Fisherman. I would fain speak a word unto thee. Too strong is the pity that overcomes me as I gaze upon thy face. I will restore to thee thy robe of feathers.

Fairy. Oh, joy! oh, joy! Give it back to me!

Fisherman. One moment! I restore it to thee on condition that thou first dance to me now, at this very hour, and in this very spot, one of those fairy dances whose fame has reached mine ears.

Fairy. Oh, joy untold! It is, then, granted to me once more to return to heaven! And if this happiness be true, I will leave a dance behind me as a memorial to mortal men. I will dance it here, that dance that makes the Palace of the Moon turn round, so that even poor transitory man may learn its mysteries. But I cannot dance without my feathers. Give them back to me, then, I pray thee.

Fisherman. No, no! If I restore to thee thy feathers, thou mayest fly home to heaven without dancing to me at all.

* Literally, the *Kariyoubiñga*, a corruption of the Indian word *Kalaviñgka*. The Japanese commentator erroneously considers *Kariyou* and *Biñga* as two separate names.

Fairy. Fie on thee! The pledge of mortals may be doubted, but in heavenly beings there is no falsehood.

Fisherman. Fairy maid! thou shamest me:
Take thy feathers and be free!

Fairy. Now the dancing maiden sings,
Rob'd in clouds and fleecy wings.

Fisherman. Wings that flutter in the wind!

Fairy. Robes like flow'rs with raindrops lin'd!
[The Fairy's dance commences.

Chorus. See the fairy's heav'nly power!
This the dance and this the hour
To which our Eastern * dancers trace
All their frolic art and grace.

I.

Chorus. Now list, ye mortals! while our songs declare
The cause that gave to the blue realms of air
The name of FIRMAMENT. All things below
From that great god and that great goddess flow,
Who first descending to this nether earth,
Ordain'd each part and gave each creature birth.

* The word "Eastern" does not refer to the position of Japan in Asia, but to that of the province of Suruga as compared to the then capital, Kiyauto.

But older still, nor sway'd by their decree,
And FIRM as ADAMANT eternally,
Stand the wide heav'ns, that nought may change
or shake,
And hence the name of firmament did take.

Fairy. And in this firmament a palace stands
Yclept the Moon, built up by magic hands;

Chorus. And o'er this palace thirty monarchs rule,
Of whom fifteen, until the moon be full,
Nightly do enter, clad in robes of white;
But who again, from the full sixteenth night,
One ev'ry night must vanish into space,
And fifteen black-rob'd monarchs take their place,
While, ever circling round each happy king,
Attendant fays celestial music sing.

Fairy. And one of these am I.
Chorus. From those bright spheres,
Lent for a moment, this sweet maid appears:
Here in Japan she lights (heav'n left behind)
To teach the art of dancing to mankind.

---

* The original Japanese word, whose derivation the Chorus thus quaintly commences by explaining, is not the firmament itself, but *hisakata*, the "Pillow-word" for the firmament, which lends itself to a similar rough-and-ready etymology. This passage has had to be paraphrased and somewhat amplified by help of the commentary in order to render it intelligible to English readers,—a remark which likewise applies to the description immediately below of the internal economy of the lunar government. The idea of the latter is taken from Buddhist sources. The great god and goddess here mentioned are the national deities Izanagi and Izanami, the creators of Japan and progenitors of gods and men.

II.

Chorus. Where'er we gaze, the circling mists are twining:
Perchance e'en now the moon her tendrils fair *
Celestial blossoms bear.
Those flow'rets tell us that the spring is shining,
Those fresh-blown flow'rets in the maiden's hair.

Fairy. Blest hour beyond compare!

Chorus.† Heaven hath its joys, but there is beauty here.
Blow, blow, ye winds! that the white cloud-belts driv'n
Around my path may bar my homeward way:
Not yet would I return to heav'n,
But here on Miho's pine-clad shore I'd stray,
Or where the moon in bright unclouded glory
Shines on Kiyómi's lea,
And where on Fusiyama's summit hoary
The snows look on the sea,

---

* The inhabitants of the far East see a cinnamon-tree in the moon instead of our traditional "man." A Japanese poetess has prettily suggested that the particular brilliancy of the autumn moon may come from the dying tints of its foliage.

† As in the following song, the Chorus frequently acts as the mouthpiece of the chief personage present on the scene. It should likewise be noted that the lyric passages contain a very great number of allusions to, and more or less exact quotations from, the earlier poetry. It has not been thought necessary to embarrass the English reader with perpetual explanatory references. By an educated Japanese none would be required.

While breaks the morning merrily!
But of these three, beyond compare
The wave-wash'd shore of Miho is most fair
When through the pines the breath of spring is playing.—
What barrier rises 'twixt the heav'n and earth?
Here, too, on earth th' immortal gods came straying,
And gave our monarchs birth,

Fairy. Who in this empire of the rising sun,
While myriad ages run,
Shall ever rule their bright dominions,

Chorus. E'en when the feath'ry shock
Of fairies flitting past with silv'ry pinions
Shall wear away the granite rock!

III.

Chorus. Oh, magic strains that fill our ravish'd ears!
The fairy sings, and from the cloudy spheres,
Chiming in unison, the angels' lutes,
Tabrets and cymbals and sweet silv'ry flutes,
Ring through the heav'n that glows with purple hues,
As when Soméiro's * western slope endues

* The Sanscrit Sumêru, an immense mountain formed of gold, silver, and precious stones, which, according to the Buddhist cosmogony, is the axis of every universe, and supports the various tiers of heaven.

The tints of sunset, while the azure wave
From isle to isle the pine-clad shores doth lave.
From Ukishíma's* slope,—a beauteous storm,—
Whirl down the flow'rs: and still that magic form,
Those snowy pinions, flutt'ring in the light,
Ravish our souls with wonder and delight.

[The Fairy pauses in the dance to sing the next couplet, and then continues dancing till the end of the piece.

Fairy. Hail to the kings that o'er the moon hold sway!
Heav'n is their home, and Buddhas, too, are they.†

Chorus. The fairy robes the maiden's limbs endue

Fairy. Are, like the very heav'ns, of tend'rest blue;

Chorus. Or, like the mists of spring, all silv'ry white,

Fairy. Fragrant and fair,—too fair for mortal sight!

---

* An alternative name for part of the shore of Miho. Mount Ashidaka, mentioned a little further on, is the eminence rising on one slope of Fusiyama, and slightly spoiling from some points of view its symmetry of form.

† Or rather Bôdhisattvas. To be a Buddha is to have attained to the highest degree of saintship, "having thrown off the bondage of sense, perception, and self, knowing the utter unreality of all phenomena, and being ready to enter into Nirvâna." A Bôdhisattva, on the other hand, has still to pass once more through human existence before it attains to Buddhaship. Readers will scarcely need to be told that "Buddha" was never the name of any one man. It is simply a common noun meaning "awake," "enlightened," whence its application to beings lit with the full beams of spiritual perfection.

Chorus. Dance on, sweet maiden, through the happy hours!
Dance on, sweet maiden, while the magic flow'rs
Crowning thy tresses flutter in the wind
Rais'd by thy waving pinions intertwin'd!
Dance on! for ne'er to mortal dance 'tis giv'n
To vie with that sweet dance thou bring'st from heav'n:
And when, cloud-soaring, thou shalt all too soon
Homeward return to the full-shining moon,
Then hear our pray'rs, and from thy bounteous hand
Pour sev'nfold treasures on our happy land;
Bless ev'ry coast, refresh each panting field,
That earth may still her proper increase yield!
But ah! the hour, the hour of parting rings!
Caught by the breeze, the fairy's magic wings
Heav'nward do bear her from the pine-clad shore,
Past Ukishíma's widely-stretching moor,
Past Ashidaka's heights, and where are spread
Th' eternal snows on Fusiyama's head,—
Higher and higher to the azure skies,
Till wand'ring vapours hide her from our eyes!

The Death-Stone.

DRAMATIS PERSONÆ.

THE SPIRIT OF THE "FLAWLESS JEWEL MAIDEN."
THE BUDDHIST PRIEST GEÑWOU.
THE CHORUS.

SCENE.—The moor of Nasu, in the province of Shimotsuke, som ninety miles to the north of Yedo.

Priest. What though the vapours of the fleeting scene
Obscure the view of pilgrims here below?
With heart intent on heav'nly things unseen,
I take my journey through this world of woe.*

I am a priest, and Geñwou is my name. Ever fixed in the seat of contemplation, I had long groaned over my imperfection in that which of all things is the most essential.† But now I see clear, and, waving in my hand the sacerdotal besom, go forth to gaze upon the world. After sojourning in the province of Michinoku, I would now fain go up to the capital, and there pass the winter season of meditation. I have crossed the river Shirakaha, and have arrived at the moor of Nasu in the province of Shimotsuke.

---

* The original of this stanza and of the next is extremely obscure, and the English translation is therefore merely tentative.
† Viz., spiritual insight.

Alas! the vapours of the fleeting scene
Obscure the view of pilgrims here below;
Strike out the hope in heav'nly things unseen,
What guide were left us through this world of
woe?

Spirit. Ah! rest not under the shadow of that stone!

Priest. What then? Is there any reason for not resting under the shadow of this stone?

Spirit. Yes; this is the Death-Stone of the moor of Nasu; and not men only, but birds even and beasts perish if they but touch it.

Seek not to die! What! hast thou not heard tell
Of Nasu's Death-Stone and its fatal spell?

I entreat thee draw not nigh unto it!

Priest. What is it, then, that maketh this stone so murderous?

Spirit. 'Tis that into it, in the olden time, entered the spirit of her who was called the "Flawless Jewel Maiden," concubine to the Emperor Toba.

Priest. Into this stone? on this far-distant road?
Methought the palace was the girl's abode.

Spirit. Verily it cannot be without reason that the story hath been handed down from the olden time.

Priest. Thine appearance and thy language seem to assure me that the tale is not unknown to thee.

Spirit. No! no! I know it but in outline. Fleeting as the dew is the memory of the maiden's fate.

Spirit. Erst through the king's abode
Priest. Proudly the maiden strode,
Spirit. Now on this des'late road
Priest. Her ghost doth dwell,
Spirit. Broods o'er the fated land,
Priest. And ev'ry pilgrim band
Spirit. Falls 'neath her murd'rous hand,
Priest. Wielding the spell!

I.

Chorus. The Death-Stone stands on Nasu's moor
Through winter snows and summer heat;
The moss grows grey upon its sides,
But the foul demon haunts it yet.

Chill blows the blast: the owl's sad choir
Hoots hoarsely through the moaning pines;
Among the low chrysanthemums
The skulking fox, the jackal whines,
As o'er the moor the autumn light declines.*

II.

Chorus. Fair was the girl,—beyond expression fair;
But what her country, who her parents were,
None knew. And yet, as in her native place,
She proudly dwelt above the Cloudy Space,†

* This stanza is an adaptation of part of an ode by the Chinese poet Peh Kü-yih.

† *i.e.*, in the Mikado's palace. The courtiers are called "the people above the clouds."

So sweetly deck'd by nature and by art,
The monarch's self soon clasp'd her to his heart.

Spirit. One day th' Imperial Majesty saw fit
To put to proof the Jewel Maiden's wit.

Chorus. Nor did she fail in ought: grave Buddhist lore,
Confucian classics of the days of yore,
Cipango's bards, the poets of Cathay,
And all the science the two realms display,—
She knew them all, nor did her answers fail
To tell of music all the wondrous tale.

Spirit. A mind so flawless in a form so fair
Deserv'd the name her lord then gave to her.

Chorus. Once the Mikado made a splendid feast
At the cool Summer Palace: ev'ry guest
That of accomplishments or wit could boast
Was bidden there,—a gay and brilliant host,
Like to the clouds, from out whose fleecy sphere
Th' imperial kindred, like the moon, shone clear.
But hark! what rumour mingles with the strains
Of liveliest music? See! the heav'nly plains
Are wrapp'd in clouds and darkness! Not a star,—
The moon not risen yet: but from afar,
Heralded by the rustling of the show'r,
The wind comes howling through the festive bow'r;
The lanterns are blown out: "A light! a light!"
Cry all the courtiers in tumultuous fright.

And lo! from out the Jewel Maiden's frame
There's seen to dart a weirdly lustrous flame!
It grows, it spreads, it fills th' imperial halls;
The painted screens, the costly pannell'd walls,
Erst the pale viewless damask of the night,
Sparkling stand forth as in the moon's full light.

Spirit. From that same hour the sov'reign monarch pin'd.

Chorus. From that same hour the sov'reign monarch pin'd
In dire disease, whose hidden cause to find
The court magician cast his curious spell,
And thus the fortune of the lots did tell:
"'Tis none but she, great Emp'ror! without doubt
That harlot is the culprit: cast her out!
Expel the fiend, who, with insidious art,
The state to ravage, captivates thy heart!"
Thus spake the seer, and in an instant turn'd
The monarch's love to hate. The sorceress, spurn'd,
Resumes her proper shape, and speeds away
To Nasu's moor, there dwelling to this day.

Priest. Thou that hast deigned to tell me this long history, who may'st thou be?

Spirit. Wherefore any longer conceal it? The demon that of old dwelt in the breast of the "Flawless Jewel Maiden," and that now inhabits the Death-Stone of the moor of Nasu is none other than myself.

Priest. Ah, well-a-day! Strange is it, but true, that the soul sunk lowest in the depths of wickedness will rise highest on the pinnacle of virtue. I will bestow on thee the priestly robe and begging-bowl.* But, prithee, reveal thyself to mine eyes in thy proper shape.

Spirit. Alas! what shame is now my portion!

In the garish light of day
I hide myself away,
  Like pale Asámá's † fires:
With the night I'll come again,
Confess my guilt with pain
And new-born pure desires.

Chorus. Dark will be the night;
But her red lustrous light
  Ne'er needs the moon.
"Wait! fear not!" she cries,
And from the hermit's eyes
Fades 'neath the stone.

[The Spirit vanishes.

Priest. 'Tis said of stocks and stones they have no soul. Yet what signifieth the text: "Herbs and trees, stones and rocks, shall all enter into Nirvâna,"‡ save that from the beginning a divine essence dwells within them? How much more, then, if I bestow on this un-

---

* For a priest to bestow his own robe on a favourite disciple is a practice of which the founder of Buddhism himself is said to have set the example.

† An active volcano situated in the province of Shinano.

‡ A quotation from the "*Hokekiyau*," or "Lotus of the Law."

happy creature the priestly robe and begging-bowl, must not her attainment of Nirvâna be placed beyond a doubt? Wherefore, with offerings of flowers and of burning incense, I recite the scriptures with my face turned toward the stone, crying:

Spirit of the Death-Stone, I conjure thee! what was it in a former world that did cause thee to assume in this so foul a shape? *

Tarry not! away! away!
From this very hour shalt thou through mine intercessions obtain Nirvâna,
From this very hour shall they gain for thee the virtues of a saint.
Hear me! hear me!

[The stone is rent asunder and the Dèmon issues from it.

Spirit. In stones there are spirits,
In the waters is a voice heard:
The winds sweep across the firmament!

Chorus. Oh, horror! horror!
The Death-Stone's rent in twain,
And lo! the demon stands reveal'd!

Priest. Strange! passing strange!
The Death-Stone's rent in twain:
O'er moor and field
A lurid glare

---

* See *infra* text and footnote p. 175.

Burns fierce. There stands reveal'd
A fox,—and yet again
The phantom seems to wear
The aspect of a maiden fair! *

Spirit. No more the mystery can be conceal'd.

I am she who first, in Ind, was the demon to whom Prince Hañzoku paid homage at the murderous mound.† In Great Cathay I took the form of Hauzhi, consort of the Emperor Iuwao; and at the court of the Rising Sun I became the "Flawless Jewel Maiden," concubine to the Emperor Toba.

Intent on the destruction of the imperial line, I assumed the shape of a fair maiden, whose presence caused the Jewel-body ‡ to languish in disease. Already was I gloating over the thought of the monarch's death, when the court magician, Abe-no-Yasunari, directed against me his powers of exorcism; he set up the many-coloured symbols § of the gods upon the altar, and gave them also into my hands:

[Here the Spirit commences a dance, which lasts till the end of the play.

---

* It is to be understood that the "Jewel Maiden" had originally been a fox, and that the moor of Nasu was her native place. Innumerable are the stories of foxes and cats assuming human shape in order to carry out their diabolical designs, and to this day the belief in the reality of such occurrences has firm hold on the minds of the less educated classes of the community.

† The translator has not been able to ascertain the details of the story to which reference is here made. The proper Chinese names of the Emperor and his consort mentioned in the next sentence are Yeo Wang and Pao Sze, who lived in the eighth century B.C. Pao Sze ruined her imperial master by her criminal luxury and folly.

‡ A phrase signifying the person of the Mikado.

§ See the note to p. 77.

Spirit. With fervent zeal the great magician prays:

Chorus. With fervent zeal the great magician prays,
And ev'ry tone with anguish and amaze
O'erpow'rs the witch, who with convulsive grasp
The holy symbols of the gods doth clasp,
And, heav'nward-soaring, flies o'er land and sea
To seek the shelter of this distant lea.

Spirit. Thereat the monarch issued his commands:

Chorus. Thereat the monarch issued his commands
To the two satraps of the neighb'ring lands: *
"Drive out," spake he, "the fiend of Nasu's moor!"
And each true liege, to make his aim more sure,
For fivescore days on dogs his arrows tried,
For to the fox the dog is near allied: †
May we not thus trace back to that command
The custom of dog-shooting in our land? ‡
Then the two satraps, arm'd with bow and spear,
And myriad horsemen brought from far and near,

* Viz., of the department of Miura and of the province of Kadzusa.

† In outward shape, not on account of the latter's possessing any of the supernatural power ascribed to the former.

‡ The sport of practising archery on dogs survived to the time of the revolution of 1868, and exhibitions of it (though rare) have been given since then, as on the occasion of the visit to Yedo of ex-President Grant in 1879. It is not cruel, at least in its modern form, as the arrows are blunted. The dogs are brought into a closed arena, and the marksmen are mounted, the horses enjoying the excitement as much as their riders. The members of the princely house of Satsuma have always been specially noted for their skill in dog-shooting.

Beat all the moor, surround its ev'ry part,
Whose rage to 'scape avails no magic art;
Swift fly the dogs, and swift the arrows fly
And, panting, stricken, I sink down and die.
But yet my ghost (though, like the morning dew
'Twas wrapt away from grosser human view)
Ceas'd not to haunt this distant des'late moor,
And from the Death-Stone wield its murd'rous pow'r,—
Till thou, great Buddha! send'st thy priest this way
To bid religion reassert her sway.
"I swear, O man of God! I swear," she cries,
"To thee whose blessing wafts me to the skies,
I swear a solemn oath, that shall endure
Firm as the Death-Stone standing on the moor,
That from this hour I'm virtue's child alone!"
Thus spake the ghoul, and vanished 'neath the stone.*

---

* The good priest's blessing does *not* seem, however, to have been effectual; for a poisonous stream still issues from the Death-Stone thrice every day.

Life is a Dream.

DRAMATIS PERSONÆ.

THE PILGRIM ROSEI.
AN ENVOY.
A MINISTER.
THE CHORUS.

SCENE.—Inn at the village of Kañtamu in China.
TIME.—Early in the eighth century.

Rosei. Lost in this pathless world of woe,
Where nothing is, but only seems,
How may the weary pilgrim know
His waking moments from his dreams?

My name is Rosei, and I dwell in the land of Shiyoku.* Though born to mortal estate,† I have hitherto idled my life away without so much as seeking to tread the Buddhist path. But they tell me that on Mount Yauhi in the land of Ibara there dwells a learned and venerable priest; and to Mount Yauhi do

---

* Shiyoku and Ibara are the Japanese names of two feudal states in ancient China, whose proper Chinese appellations are respectively Shuh and Ch'u. Kañtamu, in like manner, should be Han-tan. This latter place, in the Japanese original, gives its name to the piece. But the expression "the pillow of Kañtamu" having become proverbial in the sense rendered by Calderon's famous title, the latter has been borrowed as both more euphonious and more expressive.

† A rare boon; for, according to Buddhist views, there are many more chances in favour of one's being born as a lower animal. He who obtains this inestimable privilege should show himself worthy of it by ardently following in the footsteps of the great reformer Shiyaka Muni.

I now turn my steps to search after the one great thing needful.

Behind the clouds, in distance veil'd,
The well-known landscape fades from sight,
While endless peaks my feet have scal'd
This many a weary day and night.

Chorus. On hill and moor the setting sun
Full oft has left him desolate;
But half his course at length is run
What time he sees Kañtamu's gate.

[He arrives at the village of Kañtamu.

Rosei. What then? and is this the celebrated pillow of which I have so often heard tell? Heaven must surely have placed it in my way to bestow on me in a dream a taste of that world whose portals I am about to close for ever behind me.*

Chorus. 'Tis but a wayside inn to spend the hour
Of burning noon or wait the passing show'r;
But he would fain through some strange dream be led,
And on the magic pillow lays his head.

. . . .

Envoy. How shall I venture to address thee? I have a message for thee, Rosei.

* Not by death, but by the renunciation of all earthly vanities, which cannot but follow on my hearing the exposition of the law by the hermit of Mount Yauhi.

Rosei. Who, then, art thou?

Envoy. An ambassador sent by the Emperor of the land of Ibara to tell thee that 'tis his imperial desire to relinquish the throne in thy favour.

Rosei. Incredible! and for what cause should I be thus raised to the supreme dignity?

Envoy. Far be it from me to scan the reasons. It must doubtless be because thou possessest the capacity worthily to rule the world. But tarry not, tarry not! Deign to enter the palanquin sent to bear thee to the capital.

Rosei. What may this strange message mean?
Sure th' imperial palanquin,
Strewn with gems of radiant hue
Sparkling like the evening dew,
For my limbs was ne'er design'd.

Chorus. Strange to leave the world behind!

Rosei. But perchance of highest heav'n
To scale the heights to me is giv'n.

Chorus. Onward the palanquin they bear
In jewell'd flow'ry radiance fair;
And he (unwitting that his pow'r
Forms but the dream of one short hour)
Outsoars the clouds * to find a throne
'Mid scenes of beauty past comparison

* See note to the "Death-Stone," p. 149.

I.

Chorus. For ne'er in those old vasty halls imperial,*
Bath'd in the moonbeams bright,
Or where the dragon soars on clouds ethereal,
Was ought like this to entrance the sight:
With golden sand and silvern pebbles white
Was strewn the floor;
And at the corners four,
Through gates inlaid
With diamonds and jade,
Pass'd throngs whose vestments were of radiant light,—
So fair a scene,
That mortal eye might ween
It scann'd the very heav'ns' unknown delight.†
Here countless gifts the folk came bearing,
Precious as myriad coins of finest gold;
And there, the lesser with the greater sharing,
Advanc'd the vassals bold,
Their banners to display
That paint the sky with colours gay,
While rings the air as had the thunder roll'd.

Rosei. And in the east (to please the monarch's will),
Full thirty fathoms high,

* The references in this line and in the next line but one are to two famous ancient Chinese palaces.

† The particular heaven mentioned in the Japanese text is that entitled *Kikeñzhiyau*, or "the castle joyful to behold," the capital where Indra sits enthroned.

Chorus. There rose a silvern hill,
O'er which a golden sun hung in the sky.

Rosei. And on the western side,
O'er a gold mountain thirty fathom high,

Chorus. A silver moon did ride;—
So mote it seem as had the builder striven
To prove the poet's rhyme,*
Who sings that in th' abiding heaven
No spring and autumn mark the time,
And o'er that deathless gate
The sun and moon their wonted speed forget.

Minister. How shall I venture to address your Majesty?

'Tis already fifty years since your Majesty deigned to ascend the throne; but if you will be pleased to partake of this elixir, your imperial life may be prolonged to a millennium. Therefore have I brought hither the nectar and the patera.

Rosei. What, then, may nectar be?

Minister. 'Tis the drink of the immortals.

Rosei. And the patera?

Minister. That likewise is their wine-cup.

[After the ensuing dialogue commences the dance, which lasts until Rosei wakes from his dream.

Rosei. A thousand years this potion gives,

---

* The already often-quoted Chinese poet Peh Kü-yih.

Minister. Ten thousand springs my lord outlives.

Rosei. I the glorious sceptre swaying,

Minister. Happy multitudes obeying,

Chorus. Ev'ry town and ev'ry cot
Blest for ever in its lot.

II.

Chorus. Oh, lot immortal! rapture flow'ry fair!
Thou bear'st new blossoms still:
Each laughing guest of nectar quaffs his fill,
And bids the others share.

Rosei. Go circling round for e'er,

Chorus. Sweet cup, and on the stream securely ride!
But all too swiftly ebbs the flow'ry tide,
To stay whose burden yet the dancer yearning,—
His violet sleeve upturning,—
Waves to and fro like trembling beams of light,
While shines for e'er heav'n's silvern goblet bright.*

* The original of these verses is an extreme instance of the obscurity, logical incoherence, and many-sided application which have been noticed in the Introduction as characteristic of the style of the Japanese lyric dramas. The passage is intended to convey two distinct pictures to the mind: primarily, that of the wine-cup, whose nectar each guest would keep for himself, and regrets to see passing round and away from him. The stream of nectar, though in reality inside the cup, is thought of by the poet as outside of it, and therefore likened to a river, from a connection of ideas which leads him to allude to a festival held in the spring when goblets of wine are floated down streams on leaves and made the subject of verses. Secondarily, there is a reference to the turning round

Rosei. Haply the dews, an' they should light for ever,

Chorus. Filling the wine-cups of the flow'rs,
Might grow to be a mighty river:
But ah! what joys more fix'd are ours!
Our nectar is a living spring
Whose flow'ry waters never shall run dry,
What though we quaff for aye
Their heav'nly dews, and dance and sing
All through the day and night,
Not parting day from night,
'Mid dazzling pomp and joys more ravishing
Than e'er before were shower'd on mortal sight.

Rosei. Oh, radiant spring-time of delight,

Chorus. That never more shall end!
'Tis from the moon that fairies erst did send
This dance;* and therefore, rob'd in garments
white,
As borrow'd from a fleecy cloud,
He dances and he sings aloud,—
He sings all night for joy,
From night till morn do songs his voice employ:—
And now again 'tis surely even:

Rosei. No; midday's shining here!

---

i.e., the dancing; and the sleeve which is upturned to enable Rosei to stretch out his hand to stay the goblet, is also the sleeve which he waves in the dance. The goblet in the sky is the moon.

* See the "Robe of Feathers."

Chorus. 'Tis midday lighting up the heaven:

Rosei. No; 'tis the moonbeams sparkling clear!

Chorus. Scarce hath the spring-tide brought the
flowers,

Rosei. When scarlet leaves fall through the bowers;

Chorus. And summer hardly 'gins to reign,

Rosei. Ere snow lines all the plain.

Chorus. Spring, summer, autumn, winter, all turn
round;
No herbs so rare but strew the ground;
In one short day no flow'r but charms his sense,
And all is sweet magnificence.

III.

Chorus. So speed the hours, and now the time is o'er;
His fifty years of splendour are no more: *
'Twas all a dream, whose ev'ry shadowy grace
Must in a moment vanish into space,
Nought, as he wakes, bequeathing in their stead
Save the fam'd pillow where he laid his head.

Rosei. Mine eyelids ope and the fair vision fades:

Chorus. His eyelids ope, and all the grandeur fades:—
Astonied he sits up.

Rosei. But those sweet maids,

Chorus. In queenly garb, singing soft melodies?

Rosei. 'Twas but the zephyr rustling through the trees.

Chorus. And those vast halls of royal wealth and
pride?

---

* This does not fit in with what was said on p. 161 as to Rosei's life being prolonged to a millennium; but in a dream consistency can scarcely be expected.

Rosei. Nought but this inn where I did turn aside.

Chorus. Thy reign of fifty years?

Rosei. One hour of dreams
While in the pot a mess of millet steams.*

Chorus. Strange! passing strange!

Rosei. But he that ponders well

Chorus. Will find all life the self-same story tell,—
That, when death comes, a century of bliss
Fades like a dream; that 'tis in nought but this
Must end the monarch's fifty years of state,
Age long drawn out, th' ambition to be great,
And all that brilliant, all that joyful seems,
For there is nought on earth but fading dreams.

Rosei. Save Precious Triad! † save a suppliant soul!

Chorus. Kañtamu's pillow leads him to the goal,
Through insight to renounce all earthly things.
Thrice-bless'd the dream which such salvation brings!
LIFE IS A DREAM is what the pilgrim learns,
Nor asks for more, but straightway home returns.‡

---

* This phrase has become proverbial.

† The Sanskrit *Triratna.* It consists of the Founder of Buddhism, the Law, and the Priesthood.

‡ He had penetrated straight to the core of Buddhist doctrine, and the lessons of the holy man of Mount Yauhi would be superfluous.

NAKAMITSU.

Nakamitsu.

DRAMATIS PERSONÆ.

MITSUNAKA,* Lord of the Horse to the Emperor Murakami.
BIJIYAU, son of Mitsunaka, and still a boy.
NAKAMITSU, retainer of Mitsunaka.
KAUZHIYU, son of Nakamitsu, and foster-brother of Bijiyau.
WESHIÑ, Abbot of the great monastery on Mount Hiyei, near Kiyauto (Miaco).
THE CHORUS.

SCENE.—The Temple of Chiynuzañzhi, and my Lord Mitsunaka's palace in Kiyauto.

TIME.—Early in the tenth century.

---

* More often, following the Chinese pronunciation of the characters composing the word, called Mañjiyun. The play in the original is thus entitled, but the translator has preferred to rename it after the real hero of the piece. Mitsunaka was great-grandson of the Emperor Seiwa (died A.D. 880), and ancestor of the celebrated Minamoto family, and thereby of Yoritomo, the founder of the Shogunate. He is mentioned in the Japanese military annals as the queller of various rebellions, and may be considered as one of the warriors who were most influential in founding the mediæval feudal system.

PART I.

Nakamitsu. I am Nakamitsu, a man of the Fujihara clan, and retainer of Mitsunaka, Lord of Tada in the land of Setsushiu. Now you must know that my lord hath an only son, and him hath he sent to a certain monastery amid the mountains named Chiynuzañzhi, while I, too, have a son called Kauzhiyu, who is gone as page to young my lord. But young my lord doth not condescend to apply his mind unto study, loving rather nothing so well as to spend from morn to night in quarrelling and disturbance. Wherefore, thinking doubtless to disinherit young my lord, my lord already this many a time, hath sent his messengers to the temple with summons to return home to Kiyauto. Nevertheless as he cometh not, me hath he now sent on the same errand.

[The above words are supposed to be spoken during the journey, and Nakamitsu now arrives at the monastery.*

Prithee! is any within?

Kauzhiyu. Who is it that deigneth to ask admittance?

---

* The reader will call to mind what was said in the Introduction on the subject of the extreme simplicity which distinguishes the method of representing the Japanese lyric dramas. In accordance with this simplicity, all the changes of place mentioned in the text are indicated merely by a slight movement to and fro of the actors upon the stage.

Nakamitsu. What! is that Kauzhiyu? Tell young my lord that I have come to fetch him home.

Kauzhiyu. Your commands shall be obeyed.

[He goes to his youthful master's apartment.

How shall I dare to address my lord? Nakamitsu is come to fetch my lord.

Bijiyau. Call him hither.

Kauzhiyu. Your commands shall be obeyed.

[He returns to the outer hall and addresses his father.

Condescend to come this way.

[They go to Bijiyau's apartment.

Nakamitsu. It is long since I was last here.

Bijiyau. And what is it that hath now brought thee?

Nakamitsu. 'Tis that my lord your father hath sent me to bid your lordship follow me home without delay.

Bijiyau. Shall I, then, go without saying anything to the priests my preceptors?

Nakamitsu. Yes; if the priests be told, they will surely wish to see your lordship on the way, whereas my lord your father's commands were, that I alone was to escort you.

Bijiyau. Then we will away.

Nakamitsu. Kauzhiyu! thou, too, shalt accompany thy master.

Kauzhiyu. Your commands shall be obeyed.

[They depart from the temple, and arrive at Mitsunaka's palace.

Nakamitsu. How shall I dare to address my lord? I have brought hither his lordship Bijiyau.

Mitsunaka. Well, Bijiyau! my only reason for sending thee up to the monastery was to help thy learning; and I would fain begin, by hearing thee read aloud from the Scriptures.*

Mitsunaka. And with these words, and bidding him
read on,
He lays on ebon desk before his son
The sacred text in golden letters writ.

Bijiyau. But how may he who never bent his wit
To make the pencil trace Asáka's line †
Spell out one letter of the book divine?
In vain, in vain his sire's behest he hears:
Nought may he do but choke with idle tears.

Mitsunaka. Ah! surely 'tis that, being my child, he respecteth the Scriptures too deeply, and chooseth not to read them except for purposes of devotion. What of verse-making, then?

Bijiyau. I cannot make any.

Mitsunaka. And music?

[Bijiyau makes no answer.

Mitsunaka. What! no reply? Hast lost thy tongue, young fool?

---

* *i.e.*, the Buddhist Scriptures. The particular book intended is the "*Hoke-kiyau*," or "Lotus of the Law," the standard doctrinal work of most of the Buddhists of Japan. The reader of any modern descriptions of Japan need scarcely be told that it was only during the dark and Middle Ages that Japanese education followed this religious direction. For the last two or three hundred years the secular classics of China have had the entire forming of the national mind.

† It is said that in antiquity an ode commencing with the name of Mount Asaka was the first copybook put into the hands of children. The term is therefore now used as the "Pillow-word" for learning to write.

Chorus. Whom, then, to profit wentest thou to school?
And can it be that e'en a father's word,
Like snow that falling melts, is scarcely heard,
But 'tis unheeded? Ah! 'twill drive me wild
To point thee out to strangers as my child!
No sooner said, than out the scabbard flies
His trusty sword, and with fierce flashing eyes
Forward he darts; but, rushing in between,
Good Nakamitsu checks the bloody scene,—
Firm though respectful, stays his master's arm,
And saves the lad from perilous alarm.

Nakamitsu. Good my lord, deign to be merciful this once!

Mitsunaka. Why stayedst thou my hand? Haste thou now and slay Bijiyau with this my sword.

Nakamitsu. Your commands shall be obeyed.

[He retires into another apartment.

What is this horror unutterable? 'Tis no mere passing fit of anger. What shall I do?—Ah! I have it! I have it! I will take upon myself to contrive some plan for his escape. Kauzhiyu, Kauzhiyu, art thou there?

Kauzhiyu. Behold me at thy service.

Nakamitsu. Where is my lord Bijiyau?

Kauzhiyu. All my prayers have been unavailing to make him leave this spot.

Nakamitsu. But why will he not seek refuge somewhere? Here am I come from my lord his father as a messenger of death!

[Bijiyau shows himself.

Bijiyau. That I am alive here at this moment is thy doing. But through the lattice I heard my father's words to thee just now.

Bijiyau. Little imports it an' I die or live,
But 'tis for thee I cannot choose but grieve
If thou do vex thy lord: to avert his ire
Strike off my head, and show it to my sire!

Nakamitsu. My lord, deign to be calm! I will take upon myself to contrive some plan for your escape.— What! say you a messenger hath come? My heart sinks within me.—What! another messenger?

[These are messengers from Mitsunaka to ask whether his orders be not yet carried into execution.

Nakamitsu. Alas! each joy, each grief we see unfurl'd
Rewards some action in a former world.
Kauzhiyu. In ages past thou sinnedst;
Bijiyau. And to-day

Chorus. Comes retribution: think not then to say
'Tis others' fault, nor foolishly upbraid
The lot thyself for thine own self hast made.
Say not the world's askew! with idle prate
Of never-ending grief the hour grows late.
Strike off my head! with many a tear he cries,
And might, in sooth, draw tears from any eyes.*

* The doctrine of retribution set forth in the above lines is a cardinal point of the Buddhist teaching; and, as the afflicted Christian seeks support in the expectation of future rewards for goodness, so will the pious Buddhist find motives for resignation in the consideration of his present sufferings as the consequence of sins committed in past stages of exis-

Nakamitsu. Ah! young my lord, were I but of like age with thee, how readily would I not redeem thy life at the cost of mine own! Alas! that so easy a sacrifice should not be possible!

Kauzhiyu. Father, I would make bold to speak a word unto thee.

Nakamitsu. What may it be?

Kauzhiyu. 'Tis, father, that the words thou hast just spoken have found a lodgement in mine ears. Thy charge, truly, is Mitsunaka; but Mitsunaka's son is mine. This, if any, is a great occasion, and my years point to me as of right the chief actor in it. Be quick! be quick! strike off my head, and show it to Mitsunaka as the head of my lord Bijiyau! *

Nakamitsu. Thou'st spoken truly, Nakamitsu cries,
And the long sword from out his scabbard flies,
What time he strides behind his boy.

Bijiyau. But no!
The youthful lord on such stupendous woe

---

tence. One of their Scriptures says: "If thou wouldst know the causes in the past life, look at the effects in the present: if thou wouldst know the effects in the future life, look at the causes in the present." In such words we seem to see foreshadowed some of the most modern of philosophical doctrines.

* A little further on, Kauzhiyu says it is a "rule" that a retainer must lay down his life for his lord. Though it would be difficult to find either in the Buddhist or in the Confucian teaching any explicit statement of such a duty, it is nevertheless true that the almost frantic loyalty of the mediæval and modern Japanese was but the natural result of such teaching domiciled amid a feudal society. We may see in this drama the whole distance that had been traversed by the Japanese mind since the time of the "*Mañyefushifu*" poets, whose views of life and duty were so much nearer to those of the simply joyous and *unmoral*, though not immoral, children of nature.

May never gaze unmov'd; with bitter wail
The father's sleeve he clasps. Nought may't avail,
He weeping cries, e'en should the deed be done,
For I will slay myself if falls thy son.

Kauzhiyu. But 'tis the rule,—a rule of good renown,—
That for his lord a warrior must lay down
His lesser life.

Bijiyau. But e'en if lesser, yet
He, too, is human; neither shouldst forget
What shame will e'er be mine if I survive.

Nakamitsu. Alas! alas! and 'tis for death they strive!

Kauzhiyu. Me deign to hear.

Bijiyau. No! mine the truer word!

Nakamitsu. Ah! this my child!

Kauzhiyu. And there behold thy lord!

Nakamitsu. Betwixt the two see Nakamitsu stand:

Chorus. His own brave life, an' 'twere his lord's command,
Were freely giv'n; but now, in sore dismay,
E'en his fierce courage fades and droops away.

Bijiyau. Why heed a life my sire himself holds cheap?

Nought may thy pity do but sink more deep
My soul in wretchedness.

Kauzhiyu. Mistake me not!
Think not 'tis pity moves me; but a blot
The martial honour of our house will stain,
If, when I might have bled, my lord be slain.

Chorus. On either side 'tis infancy that pleads.

Nakamitsu. And yet how well they've learnt where duty leads!

Chorus. Dear is thy lord!

Nakamitsu. And mine own child how dear!

Chorus. But Nakamitsu knows full well that ne'er,
To save the child his craven heart ador'd,
Warrior yet dar'd lay hands upon his lord.
He to the left, the trembling father cries,
Was sure my boy, nor lifts his tear-stain'd eyes:
A flash, a moment, the fell sabre gleams,
And sends his infant to the land of dreams.*

Nakamitsu. Oh, horror unutterable! to think that I should have slain mine own innocent child! But I must go and inform my lord.

[He goes to Mitsunaka's apartment.

* Lit. "turns his child into a dream."

How shall I dare to address my lord? I have slain my lord Bijiyau according to your commands.

Mitsunaka. So thou hast killed the fellow? I trow his last moments were those of a coward. Is it not true?

Nakamitsu. Not so, my lord. As I stood there aghast, holding in my hand the sword your lordship gave me, your son called out, "Why doth Nakamitsu thus delay?" and those were the last words he was pleased to utter.

Mitsunaka. As thou well knowest, Bijiyau was mine only child. Go and call thy son Kauzhiyu, and I will adopt him as mine heir.

Nakamitsu. Kauzhiyu, my lord, in despair at being separated from young my lord, hath cut off his locks,* and vanished none knows whither.

Nakamitsu. I, too, thy gracious license would obtain
Hence to depart, and in some holy fane
To join the priesthood.†

Mitsunaka. Harsh was my decree,
Yet can I think what thy heart's grief must be
That as its own my recreant child receiv'd,
And now of both its children is bereav'd.
But 'tis a rule of universal sway
That a retainer ever must obey.

*** During the Middle Ages it was very usual for afflicted persons to renounce secular life, the Buddhist tonsure being the outward sign of the step thus taken.**

† The dramatist omits to tell us that, as we gather from the sequel, this request was not granted.

Chorus. Thus would his lord, with many a suasion fond,
Have rais'd poor Nakamitsu from despond.
Nor eke himself, with heart all stony hard,
Mote, as a father, ev'ry pang discard:
Behold him now, oh! lamentable sight!
O'er his own son perform the fun'ral rite.

PART II.

[Some time is supposed to have elapsed, and Weshiñ, abbot of the monastery on Mount Hiyei, comes down from that retreat to Mitsunaka's palace in the capital, bringing with him Bijiyau, who had been persuaded by Nakamitsu to take refuge with the holy man.]

Weshiñ. I am the priest Weshiñ, and am hastening on my way to my lord Mitsunaka's palace, whither certain motives guide me.

[They arrive at the gate, and he cries out:

I would fain crave admittance.

Nakamitsu. Who is it that asks to be admitted? Ah! 'tis his reverence Weshiñ.

Weshiñ. Alas for poor Kauzhiyu!

Nakamitsu. Yes; but prithee speak not of this before his lordship.

Weshiñ. I understand. Pray tell my lord that I am come.

Nakamitsu. Wait here, I pray thee, while I go and inform his lordship.

[He goes to Mitsunaka's apartment.

How shall I venture to address my lord? His reverence Weshiñ hath arrived from Mount Hiyei.

Mitsunaka. Call him hither.

Nakamitsu. Your commands shall be obeyed.

[He goes to the room where Weshiñ is waiting, and says :

Be pleased to pass this way.

[They enter Mitsunaka's apartment.

Mitsunaka. What may it be that has brought your reverence here to-day?

Weshiñ. 'Tis this, and this only. I come desiring to speak to your lordship anent my lord Bijiyau.

Mitsunaka. Respecting him I gave orders to Nakamitsu, which orders have been carried out.

Weshiñ. Ah! my lord, 'tis that, 'tis that I would discourse of. Be not agitated, but graciously deign to give me thine attention while I speak. Thou didst indeed command that my lord Bijiyau's head should be struck off. But never might Nakamitsu prevail upon himself to lay hands on one to whom, as his lord, he knew himself bound in reverence through all the changing scenes of the Three Worlds.* Wherefore he slew his own son, Kauzhiyu, to save my lord Bijiyau's life. And now here I come bringing Bijiyau with me, and would humbly supplicate thee to forgive one who was so loved that a man hath given his own son in exchange for him.†

Mitsunaka. Then he *was* a coward, as I thought!

* *i.e.*, the Past World, the Present World, and the World to Come. According to the Buddhist teaching, the relations subsisting between parents and children are for one life only; those between husband and wife are for two lives; while those uniting a servant to his lord or a disciple to his master endure for the space of three consecutive lives.

† This sentence, which so strangely reminds one of John iii. 16, is, like all the prose passages of these dramas, a literal rendering of the Japanese original.

Wherefore, if Kauzhiyu was sacrificed, did he, too, not slay himself?

Weshiñ. My lord, put all other thoughts aside, and, if it be only as an act of piety towards Kauzhiyu's soul,—Curse not thy son!

Chorus. As thus the good man speaks,
Tears of entreaty pour adown his cheeks.
The father hears, and e'en his ruthless breast,
Soft'ning at last, admits the fond request,
While Nakamitsu, crowning their delight,
The flow'ry wine * brings forth, and cups that might
Have serv'd the fays: but who would choose to set
Their fav'rite's bliss that, home returning, met
His grandsons' grandsons' still remoter line,
Beside the joy that doth itself entwine
Round the fond hearts of father and of son,
Parted and now in the same life made one?

Weshiñ. Prithee, Nakamitsu, wilt thou not dance and sing to us a while in honour of this halcyon hour?

[During the following song Nakamitsu dances.

---

* Literally, "the chrysanthemum wine." There is an old Chinese story of a peasant who, following up the banks of a stream bordered with flowering chrysanthemums, arrived at the mountain home of the elves and fairies. After spending a few hours feasting with them and watching them play at checkers, he set out on his homeward route, but found, to his amazement, on reaching the spot whence he had set out, that more than seven hundred years had elapsed, and that the village was now peopled by his own remote posterity. The ballad of "Urashima" at the beginning of this volume may be referred to as another way in which the Far Eastern mind has worked out the apparently world-wide tradition familiar to Europeans under the forms of Rip van Winkle and the Seven Sleepers of Ephesus.

Nakamitsu. Water-bird, left all alone
Now thy little mate hath flown,
On the billows to and fro
Flutter, flutter, full of woe!

Chorus. Full of woe, so full of woe,
Flutter, flutter, full of woe!

Nakamitsu. Ah! if my darling were but here to-day
I'd make the two together dance and play
While I beat time, and, gazing on my boy,
Instead of tears of grief, shed tears of joy!

Chorus. Behold him weep!

Nakamitsu. But the gay throng perceive
Nought but the rhythmic waving of my sleeve,

Chorus. Hither and thither flutt'ring in the wind,

Nakamitsu. Above, beneath, with many a dewdrop lin'd!

Chorus. Ah, dewy tears! in this our world of woe
If any stay, the friends he loves must go:
Thus 'tis ordain'd, and he that smiles to-day
To-morrow owns blank desolation's sway.
But now 'tis time to part, the good priest cries.
Him his disciple follows, and they rise;
While Nakamitsu, walking in their train,
The palanquin escorts; for he would fain
Last counsel give: "Beware, young lord, beware!

"Nor cease from toilsome study; for if e'er
Thy sire again be anger'd, all is lost!"
Then takes his leave, low bending to the dust.
Forward they're borne; but Nakamitsu stays,
Watching and watching with heart-broken gaze,
And, mutely weeping, thinks how ne'er again
He'll see his child borne homeward o'er the plain.

APPENDICES.

APPENDICES.

APPENDIX I.

As the severely classical character of the Japanese poetical dramas is in practice relieved by the performance between every other metrical piece of a prose comedietta, it may not be out of place to give the English reader some idea of what the latter are like. The following specimens are two taken at random from among those which the translator has himself seen acted in Yedo. The technical name of these little plays is *Nou Kiyau-Geñ*, which might be almost literally rendered as "*Folies Dramatiques*." They possess in the original a philological interest out of all proportion to the lightness of their construction, as they are almost the only source of our knowledge of the *spoken* Japanese of the Middle Ages; the written and spoken languages of Japan, as of several other Eastern countries, having all within historical times differed very considerably from each other both in grammar and in vocabulary. Their date is the same as that of the Dramatic Poems. They are, of course, acted on the same platform, and derive as little adventitious aid from scenery and stage effect.

Ribs and Skin.

(HONE KAHA.)

DRAMATIS PERSONÆ.

THE RECTOR OF A BUDDHIST TEMPLE. HIS CURATE.
THREE OF THE PARISHIONERS.

SCENE.—The Temple.

Rector.—I am rector of this temple. I have to call my curate, to make a communication to him. Curate! are you there? are you there? halloo!

Curate.—Here am I! What is your reason for being pleased to call me?

Rector.—My reason for calling you is just simply this: I, unworthy priest, am already stricken in years, and the duties of the temple service weigh heavily upon me. So, do you please to understand that, from to-day, I resign this benefice in your favour.

Curate.—I feel deeply indebted [to your reverence]. But, as I am still deficient in learning, and as, moreover, no time, however late, would seem too late to me, I beg of you to be so kind as to delay this change.

Rector.—Nothing could please me more than your most charming answer. But [you must know that], though retiring from the rectorship, I do not intend to leave the temple. I shall simply take up my abode in the back apartment; so, if there should be any business of any kind, please to let me know.

Curate.—Well, if it must be so, I will act in accordance with your august desire.

Rector.—And mind (though it will carcely be necessary

for me to say so) that you do everything in such a manner as to please the parishioners, and make the temple prosperous.

Curate.—Pray feel no uneasiness [on that head]! I will do things in such a way as to please the parishioners right well.

Rector.—Well, then, I retire without further delay. So, if there should be anything you want to ask, come and call me.

Curate.—Your commands are laid to heart.

Rector.—And if any parishioner should call, please to let me know.

Curate.—Your injunctions shall be kept in mind.—Ha! ha! this *is* delightful! To think of the joy of his ceding the benefice to me to-day, just as I was saying to myself, "When will the rector resign in my favour? when will he resign in my favour?" The parishioners, when they hear of it, are sure to be charmed; so I mean to manage in such a way as to give them all satisfaction.

First Parishioner.—I am a resident in this neighbourhood. I am on my way to a certain place on business; but, as it has suddenly begun to threaten rain, I think I will look in at the parish-temple, and borrow an umbrella. Ah! here it is! Hoy! admittance!

Curate.—Oh! there is some one hallooing at the gate! Who is that asking for admittance? Who is that hallooing?

First Par.—It is I.

Curate.—Oh! you are indeed welcome!

First Par.—It is long since I last had the honour of coming to inquire after you; but I trust that the worthy rector and yourself are still in the enjoyment of good health.

Curate.—Oh yes! we both continue well. But I must tell you that, moved by some impulse or other, my master has deigned to resign the benefice in my favour. So I pray that you will continue as heretofore to honour our temple with your visits.

First Par.—That is an auspicious event; and if I have not been [before] to offer my congratulations, it is because I was not apprised of it. Well! my present reason for calling is just simply this: I am off to-day to a certain place; but as it has suddenly begun to threaten rain, I should feel much obliged if you would kindly condescend to lend me an umbrella.

Curate.—Certainly! Nothing easier! I will have the honour to lend it to you. Please wait here an instant.

First Par.—Oh! very many thanks.

Curate.—Here, then! I will have the honour to lend you this one.

First Par.—Oh! I owe you very many thanks.

Curate.—Please always tell me if there is anything of any kind that I can do for you.

First Par.—Certainly! I will call in your assistance. [But] now I will be off.

Curate.—Are you going?

First Par.—Yes. Good-bye!

Curate.—Good-bye!

First Par.—I am much indebted to you.

Curate.—Thanks for your visit.

First Par.—Ah! well! that is all right! I will hasten on.

Curate.—As he said I was to let him know if any of the parishioners came, I will go and tell him what has passed. Pray! are you in?

Rector.—Oh! that is you!

Curate.—How dull your reverence must be feeling!

Rector.—No, I am not dull.

Curate.—Somebody has just been here.

Rector.—Did he come to worship, or was it that he had business with us?

Curate.—He came to borrow an umbrella; so I lent him one.

Rector.—Quite right of you to lend it. But tell me, which umbrella did you lend?

Curate.—I lent the one that came home new the other day.

Rector.—What a thoughtless fellow you are! Would anybody ever dream of lending an umbrella like that one, that had not even been once used yet? The case will present itself again. When you do not want to lend it, you can make an excuse.

Curate.—How would you say?

Rector.—You should say: "The request with which you honour me is a slight one. But a day or two ago my master went out with it, and meeting with a gust of wind at a place where four roads met, the ribs flew off on one side, and the skin on another. So we have tied both skin and ribs by the middle, and hung them up to the ceiling. This being so it would hardly be able to answer your purpose." Something like that, something with an air of truth about it, is what you should say.

Curate.—Your injunctions shall be kept in mind, and I will make that answer another time.—Now I will be going.

Rector.—Are you off?

Curate.—Yes.

Rector. } Good-bye! good-bye!
Curate. }

Curate.—What *can* this mean? Let my master say what he likes, it *does* seem strange to refuse to lend a thing when you have it by you.

Second Parishioner.—I am a resident in this neighbourhood. As I am going on a long journey to-day, I mean to go to the parish-temple and borrow a horse.—I will go quickly. Ah! here it is! Hoy! admittance!

Curate.—There is some one hallooing at the gate again! Who is that asking for admittance? Who is that hallooing?

Second Par.—It is I.

Curate.—Oh! you are indeed most welcome!

Second Par.—My present reason for calling is just simply this: I am off to-day on a long journey, and (though it is a bold request to make) I should feel much obliged if you would condescend to lend me a horse.

Curate.—Nothing could be slighter than the request with which you honour me. But a day or two ago my master went out with it, and meeting with a gust of wind at a place where four roads met, the ribs flew off on one side, and the skin on another. So we have tied both skin and ribs by the middle, and hung them up to the ceiling. This being so it would hardly be able to answer your purpose.

Second Par.—Why! it is a horse that I am asking for!

Curate.—Yes, certainly! a horse.

Second Par.—Oh well! then there is no help for it. I will be off.

Curate.—Are you going?

Second Par.—Yes. Good-bye!

Curate.—Good-bye! Thanks for your visit.

Second Par.—Well! I never! He says things that I cannot in the least make out.

Curate.—I spoke as my master had instructed me; so doubtless he will be pleased. Pray! Are you in?

Rector.—Oh! that is you! Is it on business that you come?

Curate.—Somebody has just been here to borrow our horse.

Rector.—And you lent him, as he fortunately happened to be disengaged?

Curate.—Oh no! I did not lend it, but replied in the manner you had taught me.

Rector.—What! I do not remember saying anything about the horse! What was it you answered?

Curate.—I said that you had been out with it a day or two ago, and that, meeting with a gust of wind at a place where four roads met, the ribs had flown off on one side, and the skin on the other, which being the case, it would hardly be able to answer his purpose.

Rector.—What *do* you mean? It was if they came to ask

for an umbrella that I told you to reply like that! [But] would anybody ever dream of saying such a thing to a person who should come to borrow a horse? Another time, when you do not want to lend it, you can make a [fitting] excuse.

Curate.—How would you say?

Rector.—You should say: "We lately turned him out to grass; and, becoming frolicsome, he dislocated his thigh, and is lying down covered with straw in a corner of the stable. This being so, he will hardly be able to answer your purpose." Something like that, something with an air of truth about it, is what you should say.

Curate.—Your injunctions shall be kept in mind, and I will make use of them next time.

Rector.—Be sure you do not say something stupid!

Curate.—What *can* this mean? To say a thing because he tells me to say it, and then, forsooth, to get a scolding for it! For all I am now my own master, I see no way out of these perplexities.

Third Parishioner.—I am a resident in this neighbourhood, and am on my way to the parish-temple, where I have some business. Well, I will make haste. Ah! here I am! Hoy! admittance!

Curate.—There is some one hallooing at the gate again! Who is that asking for admittance? Who is that hallooing?

Third Par.—It is I.

Curate.—Oh! a hearty welcome to you!

Third Par.—It is long since I last had the honour of coming to inquire after you; but I trust that the worthy rector and yourself are still in the enjoyment of good health.

Curate.—Oh yes! we both continue well. But by the way, my master, moved by some impulse or other, has deigned to resign the benefice in my favour. So I pray that you will continue to honour our temple with your visits.

Third Par.—That is an auspicious event; and if I have not been already to offer my congratulations, it is because I was not apprised of it. To-morrow being a religious anniversary [in my family], I should feel greatly obliged if our worthy rector and yourself would condescend to come [to my house].

Curate.—For myself I will come, but my master will scarcely be able to do so.

Third Par.—What! has he any other business on hand?

Curate.—No, he has no particular business on hand; but we lately turned him out to grass, and, becoming frolicsome, he dislocated his thigh, and is lying down covered with straw in a corner of the stable. This being so, he will scarcely be able to come.

Third Par.—Why! it is the rector that I am talking about!

Curate.—Yes, certainly! the rector.

Third Par.—Well! I am very sorry such a thing should have occurred. At any rate, do you, please, be so kind as to come.

Curate.—Most certainly, I will come.

Third Par.—Now I will be off.

Curate.—Are you going?

Third Par.—Yes. Good-bye!

Curate.—Good-bye! Thanks for your visit.

Third Par.—Well, I never! He says things that I cannot in the least make out.

Curate.—This time, at all events, he will be pleased. Pray! are you in?

Rector.—Oh! that is you! Is it on business that you come?

Curate.—Somebody has just been here to ask both your reverence and myself to go to him to-morrow, when there is a religious anniversary [in his family]. So I said that I would go, but that you would scarcely be able to do so.

Rector.—What a pity! I should have liked to have gone, as I just happen to be at leisure to-morrow.

Curate.—Oh! but I said what you had instructed me to say.

Rector.—I do not remember. What was it, then, that you answered?

Curate.—I said that we had lately turned you out to grass, and that, becoming frolicsome, you had dislocated your thigh, and were lying down covered with straw in a corner of the stable, so that you would scarcely be able to go.

Rector.—You really and truly went and said that?

Curate.—Yes! really and truly.

Rector.—Well, I never! You *are* an idiot! Speak as I may, over and over again, nothing seems to be able to make you understand. It was if they came to borrow a horse, that I told you to make that answer! The end of all this is, that it will never do for you to become rector. Get along with you!

Curate.—Oh!

Rector.—Won't you get along? Won't you get along? Won't you get along?

Curate.—Oh dear! oh dear! oh dear! oh dear! oh dear! But, reverend sir, for all you are my master, it is an unheard-of shame for you to beat me thus. And for all you are the man you are, you cannot be said to have been without your frolics, either,—that you cannot.

Rector.—When was I ever frolicsome? If I ever was, out with it quick! out with it quick!

Curate.—If I were to tell it, you would be put to shame.

Rector.—I am conscious of nothing that could put me to shame. If anything there be, out with it quick! out with it quick!

Curate.—Well then, I'll tell it, I will.

Rector.—Out with it quick!

Curate.—Well, then! the other day, Ichi, who lives outside the temple-gate, was here.

Rector.—And what about Ichi, pray?

Curate.—Just listen, please! Don't you call it a frolic to have beckoned to her, and then to have taken her into the bedroom?

Rector.—Insolent rascal, inventing things that I never

did, and bringing shame on your superior! After this, by the God of War with his Bow and Arrows, I shall not let you escape me!

Curate.—For all you are my master, I do not intend to let myself get the worst of it.

Both.—Ah! ah! ah! (*fighting.*)

Curate.—Has the old fool learnt a lesson? Oh! oh! I *am* glad! I *am* glad! I've beat! I've beat!

Rector.—Deary, deary me! where is he off to after having put his master in such a plight? Is there nobody there? Catch him! I won't let him escape! I won't let him escape!

Abstraction.

(ZA-ZEÑ.)

DRAMATIS PERSONÆ.

A HUSBAND. HIS WIFE. THEIR SERVANT TARAUKUWAZHIYA.*

SCENE.—A room in a private house in Kiyauto.

Husband.—I am a resident in the suburbs of the metropolis. On the occasion of a recent journey down † East, I was served [at a tea-house] in the post-town of Nogami, in the province of Mino, by a girl called Hana, who, having since then heard of my return to the capital, has followed me up here, and settled down at Kita-Shirakaha, where she expects me this evening according to a promise made by letter. But my vixen of a wife ‡ has got scent of the affair, and thus made it difficult for me to go. So what I mean to do is to call her, and tell her some pretty fable that may set me free. Halloo! halloo! are you there, pray? are you there?

Wife.—So it seems you are pleased to call me. What may it be that makes you thus call me?

Husband.—Well, please to come in.

Wife.—Your commands are obeyed.

Husband.—My reason for calling you is just simply this:

---

* Pron. Taròkaja.

† In Japan, as in England, it is usual to talk of going *up* to the Capital and *down* to the country.

‡ By some such equivalent must be rendered the Japanese term *yama no kami*, lit. "mountain spirit," which was used secondarily as the name of the wolf, and lastly transferred to the signification of "ill-tempered, overbearing wife."

I want to tell you how much my spirits have been affected lately by continual dreams that I have had. That is why I have called you.

Wife.—You are talking rubbish. Dreams proceed from organic disturbance, and do not come true; so pray don't trouble your head about them.

Husband.—What you say is quite correct. Dreams, proceeding as they do from organic disturbance, do not come true nine times out of ten. Still, mine have affected my spirits to such an extent, that I think of making some pilgrimage or other to offer up prayers both on your behalf and on my own.

Wife.—Then where shall you go?

Husband.—I mean (to say nothing of those in the metropolis and in the suburbs) to worship at every Shiñtau shrine and every Buddhist temple [throughout the land].

Wife.—No, no! I won't allow you to go out of the house for a single hour. If you are so completely bent upon it, choose some devotion that can be performed at home.

Husband.—Some devotion to be performed at home? What devotion could it be?

Wife.—Burning incense on your arm or on your head.*

Husband.—How thoughtlessly you do talk! What! is a devotion like that to suit *me*,—a layman if ever there was one?

Wife.—I won't tolerate any devotion that cannot be performed at home.

Husband.—Well, I never! You *are* one for talking at random. Hang it! what devotion shall it be? [*He reflects a few moments.*] Ah! I have it! I will perform the devotion of abstraction.

Wife.—Abstraction? What is that?

Husband.—Your want of familiarity [with the term] is but natural. It is a devotion that was practised in days of

---

* A form of mortification current in the Shiñgoñ sect of Buddhists.

old by Saint Daruma:* (blessings on him!) you put your head under what is called the "abstraction blanket," and obtain salvation by forgetting all things past and to come—a most difficult form of devotion.

Wife.—About how long does it take?

Husband.—Well, I should say about a week or two.

Wife.—That won't do either, if it is to last so many days.

Husband.—Then for how long would my own darling consent to it without complaining?

Wife.—About one hour is what I should suggest; but, however, if you can do it in a day, you are welcome to try.

Husband.—Never, never! This important devotion is not a thing to be so easily performed within the limits of a single day. Please, won't you grant me leave for at least a day and a night?

Wife.—A day and a night?

Husband.—Yes.

Wife.—I don't much relish the idea; but if you are so completely bent upon it, take a day and a night for your devotion.

Husband.—Really and truly?

Wife.—Yes, really and truly.

Husband.—Oh! that is indeed too delightful! But I have something to tell you: know then that if a woman so much as peep through a chink, to say nothing of her coming into the actual room where the devotee is sitting, the spell of the devotion is instantly broken. So be sure not to come to where I am.

---

* Bôdhidharma, the first Buddhist Patriarch of China, whither he came from India in A.D. 520. He is said to have remained seated in abstraction gazing at a wall for nine years, till his legs rotted off, and (according to an apocryphal Japanese account) to have re-appeared in Japan a hundred years after his death, being buried, on the occasion of his second decease, at a place called Katawoka in Yamato. His name is, in Japan, generally associated with the ludicrous. Thus certain legless and shapeless dolls are called after him, and snow-figures are denominated *yuki-daruma* (snow-Darumas).

Wife.—All right. I will not come to you. So perform away.

Husband.—Well, then, we will meet again after it shall have been happily accomplished.

Wife.—I shall have the pleasure of seeing you when it is over.

Husband. }
Wife. } Good-bye! good-bye! [*She moves away.*

Husband.—I say!

Wife.—What is it?

Husband.—As I mentioned before, mind you don't come to me. We have the Buddhist's warning words: "When there is a row in the kitchen, to be rapt in abstraction is an impossibility."* So, whatever you do, do not come to me.

Wife.—Please feel no uneasiness. I shall not think of intruding.

Husband.—Well, then, we shall meet again when the devotion is over.

Wife.—When it is done, I shall have the pleasure of seeing you.

Husband. }
Wife. } Good-bye! good-bye!

Husband (*laughing*). What fools women are, to be sure! To think of the delight of her taking it all for truth, when I tell her that I am going to perform the religious devotion of abstraction for one whole day and night! Taraukuwazhiya, are you there? halloo?

Servant.—Yes, sir!

Husband.—Are you there?

Servant.—At your service.

---

* Needless to say that no such text exists.

Husband.—Oh! you have been quick in coming.

Servant.—You seem, master, to be in good spirits.

Husband.—For my good spirits there is a good reason. I had made, as you know, an engagement to go and visit Hana this evening. But as my old woman has got scent of the affair, thus making it difficult for me to go, I have told her that I mean to perform the religious devotion of abstraction for a whole day and night—a good device, is it not? for carrying out my plan of going to see Hana!

Servant.—A very good device indeed, sir.

Husband.—But in connection with it, I want to ask you to do me a good turn. Will you?

Servant.—Pray, what may it be?

Husband.—Why, just simply this: it is that I have told my old woman not to intrude on my devotions; but, being the vixen that she is, who knows but what she may not peep and look in? in which case she would make a fine noise if there were no semblance [of a religious practice to be seen]; and so, though it is giving you a great deal of trouble, I wish you would oblige me by taking my place until my return.

Servant.—Oh! it would be no trouble; but I shall get such a scolding if found out, that I would rather ask you to excuse me.

Husband.—What nonsense you talk! Do oblige me by taking my place; for I will not allow her to scold you.

Servant.—Oh, sir! that is all very well; but pray excuse me for this time.

Husband.—No, no! you must please do this for me; for I will not so much as let her point a finger at you.

Servant.—Please, please let me off!

Husband.—Gracious goodness! The fellow heeds what my wife says, and won't heed what I say myself! Do you mean that you have made up your mind to brave me?

[*Threatening to beat him.*

Servant.—Oh! I will obey.

Husband.—No, no! you mean to brave me!

Servant.—Oh no, sir! surely I have no help but to obey.

Husband.—Really and truly?

Servant.—Yes, really and truly.

Husband.—[My anger] was only a feint. Well, then, take my place, please.

Servant.—Yes, to be sure; if it is your desire, I will do so.

Husband.—That is really too delightful. Just stop quiet while I set things to rights for you to sit in abstraction.

Servant.—Your commands are laid to heart.

Husband.—Sit down here.

Servant.—Oh! what an unexpected [honour]!

Husband.—Now, then; I fear it will be uncomfortable, but oblige me by putting your head under this "abstraction blanket."

Servant.—Your commands are laid to heart.

Husband.—Well, it is scarcely necessary to say so; but even if my old woman should tell you to take off the "abstraction blanket," be sure not to do so until my return.

Servant.—Of course not. I should not think of taking it off. Pray don't be alarmed.

Husband.—I will be back soon.

Servant.—Please be good enough to return quickly.

Husband.—Ah! that is well over! No doubt Hana is waiting impatiently for me. I will make haste and go.

Wife.—I am mistress of this house. I perfectly understood my partner the first time he asked me not to come to him on account of the religious devotion which he was going to perform. But there is something suspicious in his insisting on it a second time with a "Don't come to look at me! don't come to look at me!" So I will just peep through some hidden corner, and see what the thing looks like.

(Peeping.) What's this? Why, it seems much more uncomfortable than I had supposed! *(Coming in and drawing near.)* Please, please; you told me not to come to you, and therefore I had intended not to do so; but I felt anxious, and so I have come. Won't you lift off that "abstraction blanket," and take something, if only a cup of tea, to unbend your mind a little? *(The figure under the blanket shakes its head.)* You are quite right. The thought of my being so disobedient and coming to you after the care you took to tell me not to intrude may justly rouse your anger; but please forgive my rudeness, and do please take that blanket off and repose yourself, do! *(The figure shakes its head again.)* You may say no again and again, but I *will* have it off. You *must* take it off. Do you hear? *(She pulls it off, and Tarauhuwazhiya stands exposed.)* What! you, you rascal? Where has my old man gone? Won't you speak? won't you speak?

Servant.—Oh! I know nothing.

Wife.—Oh! how furious I am! Oh! how furious I am! Of course he must have gone to that woman's house. Won't you speak? won't you speak? I shall tear you in pieces?

Servant.—In that case, how can I keep anything from you? Master has walked out to see Miss Hana.

Wife.—What! *Miss* Hana, do you say? Say *Minx*, say *Minx*. Gracious me, what a rage I am in! Then he really has gone to Hana's house, has he?

Servant.—Yes, he really has gone there.

Wife.—Oh! when I hear he has gone to Hana's house, I feel all ablaze, and oh! in such a passion! oh! in such a passion! [*She bursts out crying*

Servant.—[Your tears] are but natural.

Wife.—Ah! I had meant not to let you go unhurt if you had kept it from me. But as you have told the truth, I forgive you. So get up.

Servant.—I am extremely grateful for your kindness.

Wife.—Now tell me, how came you to be sitting there?

Servant.—It was master's order that I should take his place; and so, although it was most repugnant to me, there was no alternative but for me to sit down, and I did so.

Wife.—Naturally. Now I want to ask you to do me a good turn. Will you?

Servant.—Pray, what may it be?

Wife.—Why, just simply this: you will arrange the blanket on the top of me just as it was arranged on the top of you; won't you?

Servant—Oh! your commands ought of course to be laid to heart; but I shall get such a scolding if the thing becomes known, that I would rather ask you to excuse me.

Wife.—No, no! I will not allow him to scold you; so you must really please arrange me.

Servant.—Please, please, let me off this time.

Wife.—No, no! you must arrange me, as I will not so much as let him point a finger at you.

Servant.—Well, then, if it comes to my getting a scolding, I count on you, ma'am, as an intercessor.

Wife.—Of course. I will intercede for you; so do you please arrange me.

Servant.—In that case, be so good as to sit down here.

Wife.—All right.

Servant.—I fear it will be uncomfortable, but I must ask you to put your head under this.

Wife.—Please arrange me so that he cannot possibly know the difference [between us.]

Servant.—He will never know. It will do very nicely like this.

Wife.—Will it?

Servant.—Yes.

Wife.—Well then! do you go and rest.

Servant.—Your commands are laid to heart.

[*He moves away.*

Wife.—Wait a moment, Taraukuwazhiya!

Servant.—Yes, ma'am.

Wife.—It is scarcely necessary to say so, but be sure not to tell him that it is I.

Servant.—Of course not. I should not think of telling him.

Wife.—It has come to my ears that you have been secretly wishing for a purse and a silk wrapper.* I will give you one of each which I have worked myself.

Servant.—I am extremely grateful for your kindness.

Wife.—Now be off and rest.

Servant.—Yes, ma'am.

(*Enter husband singing as he walks along the road.*)

Why should the lonely sleeper heed
The midnight bell,† the bird of dawn?
But ah! they're sorrowful indeed
When loosen'd was the damask zone.

Her image still, with locks that sleep
Had tangled, haunts me, and for aye;
Like willow-sprays where winds do sweep,
All tangled, too, my feelings lie.

As the world goes, it rarely happens even with the most ardent secret love; but in my case I never see her but what I care for her more and more:

'Twas in the spring-tide that we first did meet,
Nor e'en can I forget my flow'ret sweet.‡

Ah well! ah well! I keep talking like one in a dream,

---

* Used for carrying parcels, and for presenting anything to, and receiving anything from, a superior. The touch of the inferior's hand would be considered rude.

† Lit. "the bell late in the night," *i.e.*, the bell which was rung at the beginning of the eighth hour according to the Japanese method of reckoning time (*circa* 2 A.M.).

‡ There is a play here in the original on the name Hana, whose real signification is "flower."

and meantime Taraukuwazhiya is sure to be impatiently awaiting me. I must get home. How will he have been keeping my place for me? I feel a bit uneasy.

[*He arrives at his house.*

Halloo! halloo! Taraukuwazhiya! I'm back! I'm back! (*He enters the room.*) I'm just back. Poor fellow! the time must have seemed long to you. There now! (*Seating himself.*) Well, I should like to tell you to take off the "abstraction blanket;" but you would probably feel ashamed at being exposed.* Anyhow, I will relate to you what Hana said last night, if you care to listen. Do you? (*The figure nods acquiescence.*) So you would like to? Well, then, I'll tell you all about it:

I made all the haste I could, but yet it was nearly dark before I arrived; and I was just going to ask admittance, my thoughts full of how anxiously Hana must be waiting for me in her loneliness, saying, perhaps, with the Chinese poet: †

"He promised, but he comes not, and I lie on my pillow in
the fifth watch of the night:
The wind shakes the pine-trees and the bamboos; can it be
my beloved?"

when there comes borne to me the sound of her voice, humming as she sat alone:

"The breezes through the pine-trees moan,
The dying torch burns low;
Ah me! 'tis eerie all alone!
Say, will he come or no?"

So I gave a gentle rap on the back-door, on hearing which

---

* The meaning is that as one of the two must be under the blanket in readiness for a possible visit from the wife, the servant would doubtless feel it to be contrary to their respective positions for him to take his ease outside while his master is sitting cramped up inside,—a peculiarly uncomfortable position, moreover, for the teller of a long story.

† The lines are in reality a bad Japanese imitation of some in a poem by Li Shang-Yin (died A.D. 858).

she cried out: "Who's there? who's there?" Well, a shower was falling at the time. So I answered by singing:

"Who comes to see you, Hana dear,
Regardless of the soaking rain?
And do your words, 'Who's there, who's there?'
Mean that you wait for lovers twain?"

to which Hana replied:

"What a fine joke! well, who can tell?
On such a dark and rainy night
Who ventures out must love me well,
And I, of course, must be polite,

and say: Pray, sir, pass this way!" and, with these words, she loosened the ring and staple with a cling-a-ring, and pushed open the door with a crick-a-tick; and, while the breeze from the bamboo-blind poured towards me laden with the scent of flowers, out she comes to me, and, "At your service, sir," says she, "though I am but a poor country maid." So in we went hand in hand to the parlour. But yet her first question, "Who's there?" had left me so doubtful as to whether she might not be playing a double game, that I turned my back on her, and said crossly that I supposed she had been expecting a number of lovers, and that the thought quite spoilt my pleasure. But oh! what a darling Hana is! Coming to my side and clasping tight my hand, she whispered, saying:

"If I do please you not, then from the first
Better have said that I do please you not;
But wherefore pledge your troth, and after turn
Against me? alas! alas!

Why be so angry? I am playing no double game." Then she asked why I had not brought you, Taraukuwazhiya, with me; and on my telling her the reason why you had remained at home, "Poor fellow!" said she, "how lonely he must be all by himself! Never was there a handier lad at everything than he, though doubtless it is a case of the mugwort planted among the hemp, which grows straight without need of twisting, and of the sand mixed with the mud, which gets black without need of dyeing,* and it is his having been bound to you from a boy that has made him so genteel and so clever. Please always be a kind master to him." Yes, those are the things you have said of you when Hana is the speaker. As for my old vixen, she wouldn't let as much fall from her mug in the course of a century, I'll warrant! (*Violent shaking under the blanket.*) Then she asked me to pass into the inner room to rest awhile. So in we went to the inner room, hand in hand. And then she brought out wine and food, and pressed me to drink, so that what with drinking oneself, and passing the cup to her, and pressing each other to drink, we kept feasting until quite far into the night, when at her suggestion another room was sought, and a little repose taken. But soon day began to break, and I said I would go home. Then Hana exclaimed:

"Methought that when I met thee, dearest heart!
I'd tell thee all that swells within my breast:
But now already 'tis the hour to part,
And oh! how much still lingers unexpress'd!

Please stay and rest a little longer!" "But no!" said I, "I must get home. All the temple-bells are a-ringing." "And heartless priests they are," cried she, "that ring them! Horrid wretches to begin their ding-dong, ding-dong, ding-dong, when it is still the middle of the night!" But for all her entreaties, and for all my own regrets, I remembered that "meeting is but parting," and,

Tearing me loose, I made to go; farewell!
Farewell a thousand times, like ocean sands

* Proverbial expressions.

Untold! and follow'd by her distant gaze
I went; but as I turn'd me round, the moon,
A slender rim, sparkling remain'd behind,
And oh! what pain it was to me to part!'

(*He sheds tears.*) And so I came home. Oh! isn't it a pity? (*Weeping again.*) Ah well! out of my heart's joy has flowed all this long history, and meanwhile you must be very uncomfortable. Take off that "abstraction blanket." Take it off, for I have nothing more to tell you. Gracious goodness! what a stickler you are! Well then! I must pull it off myself. I *will* have it off, man! do you hear me?

(*He pulls off the blanket, and up jumps his wife.*)

Wife.—Oh! how furious I am! Oh! how furious I am! To hoax me and go off to Hana in that manner!

Husband.—Oh! not at all, not at all! I never went to Hana. I have been performing my devotions, indeed I have.

Wife.—What! so he means to come and tell me that he has been performing his devotions? and then into the bargain to talk about "things the old vixen would never have let drop!" Oh! I'm all ablaze with rage! Hoaxing me and going off,—where? going off where?

[*Pursuing her husband round the stage.*

Husband.—Not at all, not at all! I never said anything of the kind. Do, do forgive me! do forgive me!

Wife.—Oh! how furious I am! Oh! how furious I am! Where have you been, sir? where have you been?

Husband.—Well then! why should I conceal it from you? I have been to pray both for your welfare and for my own at the Temple of the Five Hundred Disciples * in Tsukushi.

Wife.—Oh! how furious I am! Oh! how furious I am! as if you could have got as far as the Five Hundred Disciples!

* Properly, the Five Hundred "Arhân," or personal disciples of Sâkya. The island of Tsukushi forms the south-western extremity of Japan.

Husband.—Do, do forgive me! Do forgive me!

Wife.—Oh! how furious I am! Oh! how furious I am!

[*The husband runs away.*

Where's the unprincipled wretch off to? Is there nobody there? Please catch him! I won't let him escape! I won't let him escape!

APPENDIX II.

(*See page* 77.)

FEW subjects are so difficult to obtain precise information on as this of the steps of development of the religious dances entitled Kagura and Saru-gaku. Their origin is evidently as old as that of the Japanese nation, for they are mentioned (though not by their later technical names) in the most ancient monuments of the literature, and explained by reference to the important legend of the retreat into a cave of the Sun-Goddess Amaterasu. We hear of them again in the seventh century, when a man of the name of Hada-no Kahakatsu composed several dances at the order of the Prince Regent, son of the Empress Suwiko. The name of the composer points to Corean descent, and may be thought to cast, after all, some doubt on the reality of the native origin of these entertainments. Be this as it may, they are again mentioned in the annals of the tenth and eleven centuries as being performed at the court of the Mikados, and the still existing families of actors trace their pedigree to dancers who lived at that time; but until the sudden leap taken in the fourteenth century, no advance would seem to have been made on the strings of "short odes" by which the dancers were accompanied.

The passage in the "*Kozhiki*," or "Records of Antiquity," which describes the origin and execution of the first dance in heaven may be worth quoting almost in full: *

As the Great and Grand Goddess Amaterasu sat in her

* "*Kokuñ Kozhiki*," pp. 23-26.

sacred work-room, seeing to the weaving of the Grand Garments of the Gods, [her brother Haya-Susanowo] *made a hole in the roof and dropped down through it a Heavenly Piebald Horse which he had flayed backwards, at whose aspect the maidens weaving the Heavenly Garments were so much alarmed that they died. . . . At this sight was the Great and Grand Goddess Amaterasu so much terrified that, closing behind her the door of the Rocky Abode of Heaven, she made it fast and disappeared. Then was the whole High Plain of Heaven darkened, and darkened was the Middle Land of Reed-Plains* [i.e., Japan], *in such wise that perpetual night prevailed. And the clamour of the myriad evil spirits was like unto the buzzing of flies in the fifth moon, and all manner of calamities did everywhere arise. Therefore did the eight myriad Gods assemble in a Divine Assembly on the banks of the river Amenoyasu, and bid the God Omohikane. . . . devise a plan.* [After relating how various divinities were then entrusted with the making of a mirror, the collecting of offerings, and the searching of an omen from the shoulder-blade of a stag, the text thus continues:] *And Her Grandeur Ame-no-Uzume, binding up her sleeve with the Heavenly Moss from Mount Ame-no-Kagu, and braiding the Heavenly Masaki* * *in her hair, and bearing in her hands the leaves of the bamboo-grass from Mount Ame-no-Kagu, did set a platform before the door of the Heavenly Abode, and stamp on it till it resounded, and, becoming divinely possessed, open her breasts to view, pushing the girdle of her dress down. . . . Then did the High Plain of Heaven tremble, and the eight myriad Gods did laugh in chorus. Then the Great and Grand Goddess Amaterasu was filled with amazement, and, setting ajar the door of the Rocky Abode of Heaven, spake thus from the inside: "Methought that my retirement would darken the Plain of Heaven, and that darkened would be the whole Middle Land of Reed-Plains. How, then, cometh it to pass that Ame-no-Uzume*

* Evonymus Japonicus.

thus frolics, and that all the eight myriad Gods do laugh?" To which Ame-no-Uzume replied: "If we laugh and rejoice, 'tis because there is here a Goddess more illustrious than thou." And, as she spake, Their Grandeurs Ame-no-Koyane and Futotama brought out the mirror, and respectfully showed the same to the Great and Grand Goddess Amaterasu, who, ever more and more amazed, gradually came forth from the door to gaze upon it, whereupon the God Ame-nò-Tajikarawo, who had been lying in ambush, took her by the hand and drew her out. . . . And so, when the Great and Grand Goddess Amaterasu had come forth, light was restored both to the High Plain of Heaven and to the Middle Land of Reed-Plains.

APPENDIX III.

SHORT NOTICES OF THE JAPANESE POETS AND POETESSES SPECIMENS OF WHOSE WORKS ARE GIVEN IN THE TEXT.

[*Not a little confusion is caused in Japanese, as in Chinese, literature by the variety of designations used to denote one and the same person. In the text each author has been mentioned by the individual name corresponding to our "Christian name" by which the majority of them are best known. The full names and titles are here given, the individual name being in large capitals, the surname or clan name in small capitals, and the rank or title in italics.*]

AKAHITO (YAMANOBE no * *Sukune* AKAHITO). Of this contemporary and sole admitted rival of Hitomaro (see p. 217), nothing is known but his compositions as they have come down to us in the "Collection of a Myriad Leaves." The latest bears date A.D. 736.

ASAYASU (BUÑYA no ASAYASU) was son of the better known Buñya no Yasuhide (see p. 224).

CHISATO (*Zhifu-Go Wi no Zhiyau* OHOYE no *Asoñ* CHISATO) was son of a councillor, and flourished at the end

* The word *no*, which so perpetually recurs in Japanese names, means "of." *Sukune*, like *Asoñ* and *Murazhi*, is something between a clan name and an hereditary title of nobility.

of the ninth century. He held the posts of Vice-Governor of the province of Iyo and Assistant Vice-Minister of Rites and Ceremonies, besides an office in the Department of War, and was granted a patent of nobility. He was a very fertile poet.

FUKAYABU) KIYOHARA no FUKAYABU). Of this poet no particulars have been handed down.

HASHIBITO (HASHIBITO *Kuwaugou*, *i.e.*, the Empress Consort Hashibito) was daughter of the Mikado Zhiyomei (died A.D. 641), and wife of the Mikado Kautoku (died 654).

HEÑZEU (*Souzhiyau* HEÑZEU, *i.e.*, the Buddhist Bishop Heñzeu; his original name as a layman was Yoshimine no Munesada), one of the foremost men of his time, was great-grandson of the Mikado Kuwañmu (died A.D. 806), and favourite of the Mikado Niñmiyau (died A.D. 850), to whom he seems to have been in reality tenderly attached. On the death of his patron he entered into religion, was made a bishop about A.D. 886, and died shortly afterwards. He was founder of the celebrated monastery of Kuwazañzhi, the retreat, in after years, of the melancholy Emperor Morosada. The poet Tsurayuki, who, in his celebrated preface to the "Odes Ancient and Modern," passes judgment on all the chief writers his predecessors, says of Heñzeu: "*The bishop was a skilful versifier, but in real feeling he was lacking: I might liken him to one that should conceive an artificial passion for the mere painted semblance of a maiden.*"

HIRONAHA (KUME no *Asoñ* HIRONAHA) was an official employed in the administration of the province of Koshi during the governorship of the noble poet Yakamochi (see p. 223).

HITOMARO (KAKINOMOTO *Asoñ* HITOMARO). Of this, the most celebrated of the poets of Japan, we know nothing more than can be gleaned from the notes to his poems contained in the "Collection of a Myriad Leaves," excepting the bare statement in the official annals that he died in the province of Ihami on the eighteenth day of the third moon of the year 737.* He would appear to have been a confidential retainer of Prince Hinami and afterwards of Prince Takaichi, and to have finally obtained an office in the province of Ihami, where he ended his days. Though apparently of noble origin (the "*Shiyauzhiroku*," an ancient work on pedigrees, traces his descent to the Mikado Bidatsu, who died A.D. 585), he was of low rank, a fact which is sufficiently established by the various mentions of him in the notes to the poems, and by the non-honorific Chinese character employed for the word "died" in the official notice of his decease. Legend, however, has not been content to leave so favourite a bard in obscurity, and has drawn materials from his very name where otherwise there was nothing to build on. *Kakinomoto* signifies literally "the fort of the persimmon-tree,"† and it is fabled that a warrior called Ayabe, on going one day into his garden, found standing at the foot of his persimmon-tree a child of more than mortal splendour. On being asked its name, the little creature replied, "I have neither father nor mother; but the moon and the winds obey me, and poetry is my delight." The warrior thereupon called his wife, who was as greatly charmed with the boy as her husband had been. So they took and adopted him, and named him after the tree beneath whose shade he had first been shown to them. The native author from whom this story is taken remarks: "The tale is scarcely worthy of credence; yet it is curious that the surname of Ayabe should have been handed down to this very day in the country-side where the event is said to have taken place." It is also alleged that in the vicinity of the poet's grave there grows a persimmon-tree,

* By other authorities, however, his death is placed thirteen years earlier.

† Most Japanese surnames are taken from natural objects, thus: Wisteria-Moor, Large-Estuary, Slope-of-the-Mountain. There is, therefore, nothing peculiar in Kakinomoto.

possessing, among other remarkable qualities, that of bearing fruit which are pointed and black at the end, resembling a pen in shape and colour. Akahito is the only admitted rival of Hitomaro.

ISE (ISE no *Miyasuñdokoro*, *i.e.*, Ise the imperial mistress; or ISE no *Go*, *i.e.*, the Lady Ise), so called after the province of Ise, of which her father had been governor, flourished in the latter part of the ninth and the early part of the tenth centuries. Originally maid of honour to the consort of the Mikado Uda, she was loved by the monarch himself, and gave birth to the accomplished Prince Katsura. Equally celebrated for her talents and for the gentleness of her disposition, she followed the Mikado's example in retiring from the court and the world, and, after his death, appears to have fallen into poverty, though still consulted as an authority on literary matters.

KANAMURA (KASA no KANAMURA *Asoñ*). No details of his life have been handed down. He flourished in the early part of the eighth century.

KOMACHI (WONO no KOMACHI). Less is known, though more is told, of this celebrated contemporary of the Heñzeus and the Yasuhides than of any other of the poetesses of Japan. Thus much only appears certain: that she flourished during the reigns of the Mikados Niñmiyau, Moñtoku, and Seiwa (A.D. 834 to 880), and created an immense sensation by her beauty, her talents, and the miserable old age to which her pride conducted her. In point of diction, Mabuchi, the greatest scholar of modern Japan, places her above all other female writers of verse. Tsurayuki's judgment was: "*Komachi's style is plaintive and delicate, like to a lovely woman wasted with disease.*"

KURONUSHI (OHOTOMO no KURONUSHI). Of this poet not much is known, save that he was of imperial descent, and flourished during the latter part of the ninth century. Tsurayuki, who did not appreciate his somewhat archaic manner, says of him, "*Kuronushi is clever, but his style is low. I would liken him to a woodman laden with faggots, and halting to rest under the shadow of the blossoms,*"—a dictum in which later critics are by no means disposed to acquiesce. Tradition represents him as envious and deceitful, and tells how he endeavoured to injure the reputation of the poetess Komachi by declaring that an ode which she claimed to have composed, was in reality, stolen from the "Collection of a Myriad Leaves." In order to make good this calumny, he purloined the imperial scroll of the "Myriad Leaves," and copied into it the disputed ode. But Heaven came to Komachi's rescue; for when, after adjurations to the gods in the presence of the Mikado and his court, she took water and washed the scroll, the falsely inserted verses alone were rubbed out, while the ink in which all the others were written stood firm. This tale forms the subject of one of the lyric dramas, under the title of "The Washing of the Manuscript."

MITSUNE (OHOSHIKAFUCHI* no MITSUNE) was not of noble birth. His chief distinction is that of having been one of the committee for the compilation of the "Odes Ancient and Modern."

MUSHIMARO (TAKAHASHI no *Murazhi* MUSHIMARO). Of this poet nothing is known. The denomination of *Murazhi*, however, shows him to have been of noble family.

NARIHIRA (ARIHARA no NARIHIRA *Asoñ*), the most prominent figure in the courtly annals of his age, was son of Prince Aho and of Princess Idzu, and grandson on both sides of a Mikado. He was born in A.D. 825 and died in 880, after a career in which love played the chief part. The history of some of his amours and of his exile (on account of an in-

* Commonly, but incorrectly, called OHOCHIKAFUCHI.

trigue with the Empress) to the then uncultured regions of Eastern Japan is given in the "*Ise Monogatari*," the most elegant of the prose classics of the country. Narihira is noted for his conciseness and frequent obscurity. Tsurayuki says of him, "*Narihira's stanzas are so pregnant with meaning that the words suffice not to express it. He is like a closed flower that hath lost its colour, but whose fragrance yet remaineth.*"

NIBI *Taifu* (individual name not known). No particulars of this poet have been handed down.

OHOGIMI (NUKADA no OHOGIMI) was sister-in-law to the Prime Minister Prince Kamatari, and mistress successively of the Mikados Teñji and Teñmu. She flourished in the seventh century.

OKIKAZE (FUJIHARA no OKIKAZE) held subordinate posts in the government of the provinces of Shimofusa and Sagami. We find mention of him as late as A.D. 914.

OKURA (YAMAGAMI no OKURA) was an officer in the revenue department, and afterwards Governor of the province of Chikuzeñ. He flourished during the first half of the eighth century.

SAKANOUHE (OHOTOMO SAKANOUHE no *Iratsume* *) was daughter of the Prime Minister and Commander-in-Chief Saho Dainagoñ Ohotomo no Yasumaro. She married the Viceroy of the island of Tsukushi,† and was both aunt and mother-in-law of the celebrated poet Yakamochi. Her own compositions are much esteemed by the native critics. She flourished during the first half of the eighth century.

SAKIMARO (TANABE no SAKIMARO) was an officer in

* *Iratsume* was the honorific appellation for ladies of high rank.

† Called in modern times Shikoku.

the Mikado's Wine Bureau, as we learn by a reference to him in the eighteenth volume of the "Collection of a Myriad Leaves," where he is mentioned as having been sent on business to Yakamochi, Governor of the province of Koshi, in the year 748.

SEKIWO (FUJIHARA no SEKIWO) seems to have held the posts of President of the Board of Rites, Chief Lay Official of the Shiñtau temples at Ise, and Governor of the province of Shimotsuke during the reign of the Mikado Buñtoku (A.D. 851–858).

SHIYAUMU* (SHIYAUMU *Teñwau*, AME-SHIRUSHI-KUNI-OSHI-HIRAKI-TOYO-SAKURA-HIKO no *Mikoto*) was the forty-sixth Mikado, and reigned from A.D. 724 to 756. As stated in the Introduction, it is to the reign of this prince that the "Collection of Ten Thousand Leaves" must almost certainly be referred.

SOSEI (SOSEI *Hofushi*, *i.e.*, the Buddhist priest Sosei; his original name as a layman was Yoshimine no Hironobu) flourished in the latter part of the ninth century, and is said to have been the son of the more illustrious poet, the Buddhist Bishop Heñzeu, who had been married prior to his entry into religion. Sosei himself was abbot of the monastery of Riyau-iñwiñ at Isonokami, a famous religious centre in the province of Yamato.

TADAMINE (NIBU † no TADAMINE). Nothing certain

* Mikados are always known, not by their personal, but by their posthumous names, for which reason, and on account of the unmanageable length of the personal name, the posthumous name has been adopted in the text, and is here, for the sake of clearness, printed in small capitals. *Teñwau* is the designation of the imperial dignity, meaning, as it does literally, "Emperor of Heaven." *Mikoto* is equivalent to our title of Highness or Majesty, and is also applied to the gods.

† Commonly, but incorrectly, called MIBU.

is known of Tadamine but the fact of his having been one of Tsurayuki's three coadjutors in the work of editing the "Odes Ancient and Modern." He is said to have died in 965 at the age of ninety-nine.

TOSHIYUKI (FUJIHARA no TOSHIYUKI *Asoñ*), during his short life of seven-and-twenty years held successive important posts in the Imperial Guard, and died in or about A.D. 907. To his other talents he joined the, in Japan, highly prized one, of caligraphy.

TSURAYUKI (KI no TSURAYUKI). The noble house of Ki claimed descent from the Mikado Kaugeñ through Takeu-suchi Sukune, the Methusaleh of Japan. Tsurayuki's own history is but a catalogue of the important official posts to which he was raised, and of brilliant literary achievements. He was successively head of the Official Department of Literature, Private Secretary in Chief to the Mikado, Governor of the province of Tosa, Minister for Foreign Affairs, and Supervisor of the Imperial Constructions. He died in A.D. 946 at the age of sixty-two. Though much admired as a poet,* his chief glory is that of having been the first prosaist in his native tongue, all prose compositions up to that time, excepting a few liturgies and edicts, having been made in Chinese, or what passed for such. The prose works by which he is best known are, the "*Tosa Niki*," a charmingly simple and lifelike account of his voyage home by junk from Tosa to the capital, and the extremely elegant Preface to the "Collection of Odes Ancient and Modern," the gathering together and editing of which was intrusted to him and to three other literary men of the period, by the Mikado Daigo.

YAKAMOCHI (*Chiyuunagoñ* OHOTOMO no *Sukune* YAKAMOCHI), the most favourite of the ancient poets with the

* The present writer considers him to be, in point of versification, the sweetest of all the poets of Japan.

modern Japanese, was son of the Prime Minister Tabiudo and grandson of the Prime Minister Yasumaro. He was successively Governor of the province of Koshi, and Viceroy and Commander-in-Chief of the then unsettled country in the east and north of the Empire. He died in A.D. 785.

YASUHIDE (BUÑYA no YASUHIDE) was vice-director of the Imperial Bureau of Fabrics, and likewise occupied a post in the administration of the province of Sagami. He flourished during the latter part of the ninth century.

YOSHIKI (WONO no YOSHIKI) is said to have been an excellent Chinese scholar, and to have died in A.D. 902.

YUKIHIRA (*Chiyuunagoñ* ARIHARA no YUKIHIRA *Asoñ*) was half-brother to the more celebrated Narihira, whom he surpassed in practical ability. He died in A.D. 893 at the age of seventy-five, after having occupied distinguished posts under six successive Mikados.

ZHIYOMEI * (ZHIYOMEI *Teñwau*, TAMURA or OKI-NAGA-TARASHI-HI-HIRO-NUKA no *Mikoto*) was the thirty-fifth Mikado, and reigned from A.D. 629 to 641.

---

* See note to SHIYAUMU.

APPENDIX IV.

INDEX OF FIRST LINES TO FACILITATE REFERENCE TO THE JAPANESE ORIGINALS IN THE "COLLECTION OF A MYRIAD LEAVES."

[The *pages* referred to are those of the "*Riyakuge*" edition.]

N.B.—The references to the originals of the "Odes Ancient and Modern" are given in the text. The Japanese names of the four lyric dramas there translated are "*Ha-goromo*," "*Setsu-shiyau-seki*," "*Kañtamu*," and *Mañjiyuu*," by which they will easily be found in any complete edition. The names of the writers of these plays are not to be ascertained, owing to a peculiar Japanese custom of attributing to the head of the clan of lyric actors at any given time, the authorship of all such pieces as came out under his auspices.

THE END.

For Product Safety Concerns and Information please contact our EU representative GPSR@taylorandfrancis.com Taylor & Francis Verlag GmbH, Kaufingerstraße 24, 80331 München, Germany

Printed and bound by CPI Group (UK) Ltd, Croydon, CR0 4YY
11/04/2025
01844009-0003